# The Two-Fold Knowledge

# The Two-Fold Knowledge

*Readings on the Knowledge of Self &
the Knowledge of God*

Selected & Translated from the Works of
Saint Bernard of Clairvaux

by
Franz Posset

WIPF & STOCK · Eugene, Oregon
*2018*

Wipf and Stock Publishers
199 W 8th Ave, Suite 3
Eugene, OR 97401

The Two-Fold Knowledge
Readings on the Knowledge of Self and the Knowledge of God
Selected and Translated from the Works of Saint Bernard of Clairvaux.
Collected Works Volume 1.
By Posset, Franz
Copyright©2004 by Posset, Franz
ISBN 13: 978-1-5326-4589-1

Publication date 6/15/2018
Previously published by Marquette University Press, 2004

# Preface to the 2018 Reprint Edition

*The Two-Fold Knowledge*, as volume 1 of my Collected Works, has the function of whetting the reader's appetite for taking a closer look at Saint Bernard of Clairvaux and his insights into a timeless, Christ-centered spirituality and theology. *The Two-Fold Knowledge* wants to facilitate the access to Bernard, who has been called not only a "difficult saint," but also a "difficult writer." Simultaneously, besides introducing Bernard's thought-world to the reader in the twenty-first century, the given text selections are meant to prepare for the crossing of the bridge across the Late Middle Ages and the early Renaissance era toward Martin Luther. Or, in other words, *The Two-Fold Knowledge* wants to lead directly to Luther, whose deep indebtedness to Bernard is investigated in greater detail in vol. 2 of my Collected Works, *Pater Bernhardus*.

To Luther, the friar, the ex-friar, and the reformer, Saint Bernard was always his "Father Bernard"—that is, for his entire career, and not only as a young friar at Erfurt. A few years before his death, Luther declared in a sermon on 14 September 1538: "[Bernard] is the only one worthy to be called *Pater Bernhardus* and to be studied diligently." This conviction has something to do with the insights Luther had gained and expressed almost two decades earlier, namely in his second lectures on the Psalms, about the connection between the knowledge of self and the knowledge of God: "According to Bernard, knowledge of self without the knowledge of God leads to despair" (see Introduction, 19). Luther must have had in mind certain passages in Bernard's Sermons 36, 37, and 38 on the Canticle (see text selections, pp. 46-50).

The selections in the *Two-Fold Knowledge* are often very curt and without the provision of the immediate or the wider context—something which readers might miss. However, the source references given with each of the text selections should make it relatively easy for the interested reader to look up the entire sermon or document from which they are taken.

Besides the text selections there are numerous pictures incorporated showing one single motif, namely Christ Crucified embracing Bernard from the cross with both arms, which traditionally is called the *Amplexus Bernardi* motif. The Bernard iconography of the Middle Ages comprises almost one thousand extant images of him—that is, up to Luther's time, ca. 1530 (James France, *Medieval Images of Saint Bernard of Clairvaux*, 2007). From among them, the *Amplexus Bernardi* is one of the most often shown. In the fifteenth century, pictorial representations of Saint Bernard were so popular that they found dissemination well beyond the monasteries of Bernard's own Cistercian Order. It so happened that Luther's confreres in the Augustinian (!) friary at Nuremberg had an altar painting commissioned in about 1487 with exactly that motif (see the reproduction in my *Pater Bernhardus*, Plate 13; today in the Bavarian State Gallery, Munich).

A reader of the *Two-Fold Knowledge* might expect to see primarily the medieval images of the *Amplexus Bernardi* as an accompaniment to the medieval texts selected here. However, in order to drive home the point that Bernard's life and works are of great interest throughout the centuries, from medieval to modern times, the picture-selections for the *Two-Fold Knowledge* are taken not from the time of the Middle Ages, but from the time after Luther, i.e. from the late sixteenth century and up to the present time. Bernard, thus, in a way, is deliberately taken out of his historical connections in order to demonstrate his tremendous "impact" (what the Germans call *Wirkungsgeschichte*) for every age, including the twenty-first century.

The pictures may be inspiring to some, but distracting to others. Those who may feel distracted should simply ignore them. The historian might be distracted, especially when s/he is familiar with the fact that the *Amplexus Bernardi* is based on legend and might represent a common, yet perhaps a lop-sided understanding of Bernard's Christology. Nevertheless, the *Amplexus Bernardi* images may assist and direct personal meditation. Visitors at monastic book stores probably favor the *Two-Fold Knowledge* exactly for that reason. Soon after its first edition, Brother Patrick Hart shared the observation with me that at their monastic bookstore and gift shop the book is "doing well," which—in terms of a ripple effect—helps explain that the book is now out of print and that a reprint is in order in 2018.

The texts offered here can stand on their own merits. They allow Bernard to lead the way, without imposing an artificial structure on his words, which is a particularly enjoyable feature of this collection (Daniel M. La Corte, book review, 2006). Therefore, the book can be read for edification or in a college classroom when Bernard of Clairvaux and his thought-world are to be introduced.

Franz Posset
Beaver Dam, Wisconsin, Thanksgiving 2017

# Table of Contents

| | |
|---|---:|
| Preface to the 2018 Reprint Edition | 3 |
| Corrections | 8 |
| Foreword by John R. Sommerfeldt | 9 |
| Editor's Preface | 13 |
| Introduction | 17 |
| 1. Know yourself | 43 |
| 2. Know yourself as Christ's beast of burden | 54 |
| 3. Know your tribulations | 59 |
| 4. Know the Word of God | 67 |
| 5. Knowledge that comes from the school of God | 73 |
| 6. Know the true godliness | 77 |
| 7. O Lord it is hard, but smart, to be humble | 83 |
| 8. Know God in Christ | 93 |
| 9. This is my philosophy: to know Jesus and him Crucified | 101 |
| 10. Accusation of self; Justification by God | 109 |
| 11. Know that it is enough for merit to know that merits are not enough | 115 |
| 12. Know how to shepherd | 123 |
| 13. Know your direction and your spiritual progress | 129 |
| Epilogue | 135 |
| List of Illustrations | 151 |

# Corrections

p. 14, last line: accepting the original manuscript
p. 25, line 11: delete: footnote 50
   line 23: add: Fig. 32
p. 28, line 8 from bottom: delete capital letter, I, after the parenthesis
p. 37: the font size of note 49 needs to conform to the rest of the size of the notes;
   within note 57, delete the letter, É, after the year 1990
p. 39, within note 89: the German word is: ökumenische
p. 104, line 13 from bottom: . . . the insults, the spitting, the blows
   line 4 from bottom: nos. 1-4
p. 105, in the section 'Christ Alone': [Gen 2:9]; and: nos. 5-6
p. 111, last line: should be Roman numeral XIV
p. 125, line 5 from bottom: 67:34
p. 127, line 11: John 19:11
p. 128, line 14: Pastor
p. 133, line 7 from bottom: . . . step of the spiritual exercise
p. 140, with Fig 25: Glass Window
p. 141, line 1: known from
p. 151, Fig. 1 is replaced on the new book cover of 2018 with the image from the Scriptorium of the Cistercian Abbey of Zwettl, Austria, dated ca. 1189.

# Foreword

We celebrated St. Bernard's 850th birthday on 20 August 2003, for it was on that date in 1153 that he died. By medieval reckoning, Bernard's death was his second rebirth. He was probably born in 1090, and surely baptized shortly thereafter, in his first rebirth. His birth in heaven was thus his second rebirth. We celebrate Bernard's feast for two reasons: first, because of his overwhelming importance for his own age, and, secondly, because of his lasting influence on the spirituality of the western Church and, thus, on ours.

Bernard of Clairvaux was the leader of Christendom in the first half of the twelfth century in so many aspects of the life of the time that it would be difficult to find a parallel in any similar period. Perhaps more than any other single event in his life, Bernard's role at the Council of Etampes reveals the extent of his influence on contemporary society. At this council Bernard was instrumental in settling the papal schism of 1130, and his conviction helped win France for Innocent II. This was but preliminary to Bernard's campaign in England, Germany, Italy, and Sicily, a campaign pursued successfully through letters, travels, councils, and disputations. In an age in which religion is as important as it surely was in the twelfth century, the person who is instrumental in choosing the head of the institutional expression of that religion is a person of great power. And from 1130 to his death in 1153, Bernard did not cease to play a role of primary significance in the affairs of his world.

Bernard's role in launching in 1146 the Second Crusade is well known. His preaching and letters aroused the European conscience to the point that he could write to Pope Eugenius III:

> You have commanded, and I have obeyed. And the authority of your command has made my obedience fruitful. Since "I have announced and have spoken, [the soldiers of the Cross] have increased beyond number." Cities and castles are emptied, and now seven women can hardly find one man to hold—so much so that everywhere there are widows whose husbands are still alive.

Due in large part to Bernard's efforts, a vast army of men took the cross and set out for the East.

Bernard also had a strong voice in the direction of the society of his time through his influence on the regularly constituted leaders of that society. Bernard was the preceptor of popes and the conscience of kings. Many of his over 500 letters which we still have and read are addressed to popes, patriarchs, cardinals, archbishops, bishops, abbots, canons, and other clergy-exhorting them to fulfill their ministry according to the pattern of Christian virtue. Bernard admonished and praised lay leaders as well; he did not hesitate to write or preach to emperors, kings, and princes as the occasion seemed to demand. The administration of early twelfth-century society was thus subject to Bernard's surveillance. But that was not all.

Bernard also powerfully influenced significant aspects of the intellectual and spiritual life of Europe. Many scholars have demonstrated Bernard's great contribution to contemporary theology and his influence on its development. A telling index to Bernard's influence on intellectual and spiritual life is the number of manuscripts of his works which circulated throughout Europe during his own lifetime, some 1,500 of which have survived to our own day. In short, Bernard was a leader in so many aspects of early twelfth-century culture that it is impossible to examine his age without studying him.

Bernard's leadership leads one to ask: how is it that a monk could play such a role? How is it that a man dedicated to withdrawal from the world could have so much influence on the world? My conviction is that Bernard could lead Europe to a crusade, powerfully influence who its leaders were to be and how they were to act, and help shape the spiritual life of its inhabitants because his life embodied so many ideals of his age, some of which had not crystallized until his coming. The ideals of early twelfth-century Europe were largely unified around spiritual values. Thus it was possible for one man, who as a monk embodied those ideals most perfectly-at least so it was thought-to give expression to the values of his age. Because of his genius, Bernard was able to explicate forcefully the ideals and values implicit in his society's choice of him as its leader.

There is another, still more important reason for celebrating and reading Bernard, for he led a twelfth-century revolution in the way

Christians viewed themselves and their spiritual life. And this revolutionary spirituality was rediscovered by scholars in the years before Vatican II and influenced mightily the decisions of that council.

Early Christian thinkers adopted a Platonic way of viewing their universe. This view saw matters as literally next to nothing, and thus the spiritual life was seen a process of rejecting all that is material and hence "worldly." Hence, a rigorous asceticism-involving extreme fasting, sleeplessness, and the rejection of sexual impulses-was widely practiced in an effort to mortify (literally, to kill) the body. The early Christian universe was created and governed by a harsh and demanding God whose chief attribute was justice.

Bernard's universe was created out of love and is informed by God's love and mercy. Matter is not evil, and the human body is as important as the human soul in the process of sanctification. So important is the body that Bernard thinks that we shall not be completely satisfied even by heaven until we are reunited with the body. For Bernard, love is imperative and friendship is essential. And married life is not merely a means of reproduction but a glorious path to perfection.

All this prompts us to read Bernard. We are grateful to Franz Posset for his excellent selections, well chosen to introduce us to the "honey-tongued doctor" who was Bernard of Clairvaux.

John R. Sommerfeldt
University of Dallas
31 May 2002

# Editor's Preface

My first encounter with Bernard of Clairvaux took place during my research for my dissertation on Martin Luther's understanding of Christ. It was this Reformer who led me to Saint Bernard, as I realized that Luther was heavily influenced by this monastic-theological author who functioned for him as a mentor. Surely, I had heard of Bernard before; but, as far as I remember, I never heard any of my professors of theology mention Bernard being of any significance in and for the history of theology, or Bernard being of significance similar to Thomas Aquinas for theology and Church. Bernard was simply a figure of past, medieval church history. Only because of Luther's high regard for Bernard was I induced to take a closer look at this medieval monk and his works. And I do not regret it, as I have greatly benefited from the study of Bernard's sermons in particular, which I read, at first, through the lenses of Luther, the great preacher of God's grace. However, my reading of Bernard became much broader as time went by. Nevertheless, I think that Luther's view of Bernard is the essential core of Bernard as a theologian, and thus I hope that this anthology incorporates all the major aspects of Bernard's insights into the knowledge of God and of self.

Not seldom Bernard preaches and teaches on grace alone, humility alone, faith alone, Christ alone, and shepherding in terms of preaching the Gospel alone. This concentration on the 'alones' made his insights very attractive to most of the major reformers of the sixteenth century. Their references and quotations, much investigated in recent years,[1] provide this compiler considerable assistance in arranging the excerpts in this anthology. However, it was not only the reformers of the sixteenth century who were impressed with Bernard's Christ-centered view; the generations before them were equally taken with Bernard's teaching.

People in the Late Middle Ages appear to have cherished the legend and the image of Bernard under the cross of Christ and being embraced by the Crucified.[2] This iconographic motif, though based on legend, best summarizes Bernard's philosophy, theology and spirituality. Not only the generations before the Reformation, but also the later generations of modern times appear to have cherished this particular motif as, for instance, Francisco Ribalta (1550-1628) shows with his painting of Christ embracing Bernard from the cross, a creation of 1582.

Paul Diemer has referred to this painting in the introduction of his anthology of Bernard texts in this way: 'The painting expresses the culmination of a relationship which according to Bernard's teaching was at the heart of the Christian/monastic life.'[3] Michael Casey has used Ribalta's painting for the cover of his book *Athirst for God: Spiritual Desire in Bernard of Clairvaux's Sermons on the Song of Songs*,[4] as did Bernardin Schellenberger in his collection of Bernard texts in German.[5] The embrace motif, which first emerged around 1320 in southern Germany[6] is so impressive that artists of the late twentieth century have revived it. Samples from the history of the motif from the late sixteenth to the late twentieth century accompany the text selections here. It is my hope that the illustrations will be an inspiration to the reader/viewer. They are meant not merely as accompaniment to the texts; they have the purpose of providing a sense of the Christ-centered philosophy and devotion which Bernard favored and which inspired the Bernard iconography throughout the centuries. Even Bernard's devotion to the Virgin Mary is christocentric.[7]

I have given careful thought in re-translating the selected texts from the critical edition of Bernard's works.[8] For the purpose of control I have consulted the new German edition (published between 1990 and 1999),[9] and those works of Bernard that up to this point are available in the Cistercian Fathers series of Cistercian Publications. Bernard's eloquent Latin cannot always be recreated in a translation. But I hope this anthology will inspire not only those who read it for edification, but also scholars who may be led to investigate Bernard further (and perhaps in his original Latin). The reader should note that the references to the Book of Psalms follow the Vulgate's numbering. Abbreviations normally follow the Cistercian Studies Style Sheet.

I want to thank Professor John R. Sommerfeldt for his helpful hints in improving the translations and for his Foreword, Professor Andrew Tallon of Marquette University Press for accepting the manuscript for publication, and the numerous monasteries, libraries, and archives that have made me aware of, and helped me locate, the *Amplexus* images for my collection, especially Sr. Dr. Mechthild Bernart OCist, now Abbess, of the Abbey of St. Josef in Thyrnau in Bavaria, and Fr. Dr. Gabriel Hammer at the abbey of Cistercian nuns in Oberschönenfeld, also in Bavaria.

As I began to investigate and publish articles on Saint Bernard in 1987, the editors of the monastic journal *Cistercian Studies Quarterly* graciously accepted most of my articles. I, a Catholic layman writing on Bernard the monk, am very grateful to these monastic editors and to their boards of advisors for accepting a layman's view on Bernard in the pages of this journal. I am grateful too for their help in shaping and sharpening both my arguments and my second language, English. To them this book is dedicated.

Beaver Dam, Wisconsin<br>On the Feast of St. Bernard, 20 August 2004

## Notes

[1] See, for example, Theo Bell, *Divus Bernhardus: Bernhard von Clairvaux in Martin Luthers Schriften* (Mainz: Philipp von Zabern, 1993). Dennis E. Tamburello, *Union with Christ: John Calvin and the Mysticism of St. Bernard* (Louisville: Westminster John Knox Press, 1994). Anthony N. S. Lane, *Calvin and Bernard of Clairvaux* (Princeton: Princeton Theological Seminary, 1996); and my own studies on Luther and Bernard, in particular *Pater Bernhardus: Martin Luther and Bernard of Clairvaux* (Kalamazoo: Cistercian Publications, 1999).

[2] See Franz Posset, 'The Crucified Embraces Saint Bernard: The Beginnings of the *Amplexus Bernardi*,' *Cistercian Studies Quarterly* 33 (1998) 289-314; idem, 'The Dissemination of a Cistercian Motif in the Late Middle Ages,' with a catalogue of representations of the *Amplexus Bernardi*, in *Cîteaux*, forthcoming (with more than 50 known images from about 1320 to 1520 being listed).

[3] Paul Diemer, *Love Without Measure: Extracts from the Writings of St Bernard of Clairvaux* (Kalamazoo: Cistercian Publications, 1990) xi.

[4] Kalamazoo: Cistercian Publications, 1987.

5. *Bernard of Clairvaux: Rückkehr zu Gott* (Düsseldorf: Patmos, 2001).
6. See Posset, 'The Crucified Embraces Saint Bernard,' 300-02.
7. See Frederick M. Jelly, 'The Christocentric Devotion to Mary in Saint Bernard of Clairvaux,' *Cistercian Studies Quarterly* 34 (1999) 89-105.
8. Jean Leclercq et al. (eds.), *Sancti Bernardi Opera*, 8 volumes in 9 (Rome: Editiones Cistercienses, 1957-1977), quoted as SBOp. When quoting SBOp, the volume number appears before the colon, the page number after the colon, followed by the number of lines; for example: SBOp 1:2,3-4 means volume 1, page 2, lines 3-4.
9. German/Latin edition by Gerhard B. Winkler, *Bernhard von Clairvaux: Sämtliche Werke*, 10 volumes (Innsbruck: Tyrolia, 1990-1999).

# Introduction

What would make the writings of a monk who died 850 years ago attractive still today? And, no doubt, he is an attractive author.[1] His attractiveness lies in his insights into spiritual matters[2] as a 'pre-critical' scholar of the Scriptures.[3] However, Bernard is of great interest also for philosophers of the caliber of Maurice Blondel (1861-1949).[4] What makes Bernard of Clairvaux 'present to the centuries,' is the 'total integrity and practicality,' the 'depth and sublimity' of his spirituality, exemplified by a life journey which he was able to communicate in his 'exceptionally beautiful writings'. However, 'the exquisite beauty of his carefully crafted Latin is largely lost in translation'.[5] Indeed, it was his elegant literary Latin that has guaranteed his effectiveness as a theological and spiritual author. He was a man of letters, a great writer by any standard. Bernard the monk did not renounce the art of good writing on important matters. 'He writes about things that are at the very heart of human and Christian experience.'[6]

His literary production began when he was about thirty years of age. Between 1120 and 1125, he wrote four *Homilies in Praise of the Blessed Virgin Mary*. Around 1125, he wrote the treatises on the *Steps of Humility and Pride* and his *Apologia to Abbot William*. In 1127/28, were written some of his so-called letters, actually treatises such as *Letter* 42 on the duties of bishops and *Letter* 77 on baptism. In 1130, he expanded on his *Letter* 11 on the steps toward loving God and made it the treatise *On the Necessity of Loving God*. His letters were collected and circulated by his secretaries. The earliest letter is *Letter* 441, probably written to the prior of Clairvaux, on accepting a young man into the monastery. In 1128, he wrote *On Grace and Free Choice* and *In Praise of the New Knighthood*.

In mid-career so-to-speak (about 1135) he started his *Sermons on the Song of Songs* and realized some twenty four of them. His *Letter* 190 on the errors of Peter Abelard was written in 1139. In 1139/40, he wrote his *Sermons on Psalm 90*, his *Sermon to Clerics on Conversion*, and, in 1141 or later, *On Precept and Dispensation*. The Sermons 25 to 79 were added to his Song commentary in these years. The *First Sermon on the Annunciation* was written probably in 1141, and the *Third* in

1150. The older Bernard worked on his book for Pope Eugene, *On Consideration* (1148/53) and *On the Life of St. Malachy* (1148/50). Shortly before his death he finished his *Sermons on the Song of Songs* 80 to 86. Most of the sermons in the large body of *Sermons for the Liturgical Year* and the *Occasional Sermons* cannot be dated. These texts are and were meant to be timeless and of general validity.[7]

All these texts are extant not only because their author was an outstanding personality with international reputation, 'a prophet,'[8] and a 'great medieval thinker,'[9] but also because Bernard himself made sure that his works were handed down to later generations. At the end of his life he carefully improved almost all his works. He had written well and wanted to write even better. However, one may also suspect that he did not rewrite every word himself, just as it is likely that the polished sermons we read today are not necessarily identical with his actual preaching.[10]

Bernard was one of those great men who are met either with animosity or admiration.[11] Along with Martin Luther[12] I am in the camp of Bernard's admirers. And I am challenged to discover a way of presenting selections from his works that are most impressive to me, being mindful that Bernard may be read from the perspective from which Luther read him, that is, not so much as a mystic but as a model preacher. The Dutch theologian, Theo Bell, inspired by his studies of Luther and Bernard, recently published in Dutch sixteen text selections, mostly from Bernard's sermons.[13]

G. R. Evans had arranged the text selection for *The Classics of Western Spirituality* in the order of a spiritual pilgrimage from the 'Conversion of Clerics,' via the 'Steps of Humility and Pride' and the 'Consideration' of self and of God toward the ultimate goal of 'Loving God'.[14] Among contemporary Cistercians nuns and monks, collections of excerpts are usually arranged from the perspective of Bernard 'the Lover' and his teaching on love.[15] One Cistercian expert has proposed a reading program based on the chronological order of his works.[16] These are all good choices.

My approach is somewhat different: Knowledge of self as a continuing philosophical issue is only my starting point.[17] The goal here is to go beyond self-knowledge toward the knowledge of God. As far as I can see, no Bernard-anthology has ever been presented with the selection principle of 'knowledge,' that is, knowledge of self and of God (which I offer here). This observation may be surprising, especially because the early twentieth-century Nestor of Bernardine studies, Étienne Gilson, perceived in Bernard's use of the ancient Greek precept 'Know yourself' one of the clues to an understanding of his teaching, as another, later Nestor, Jean Leclercq, noted in 1976 in his work on the Cistercian spirit.[18]

Knowledge of self and of God is not only a philosophical issue. It is also an eminent topic of Reformation theology. John Calvin (1509-1564) in his *Institutio* of 1539 starts with this sentence: 'Well-nigh the sum of sacred doctrine consists in these two parts, the knowledge of God and the knowledge of ourselves,' and he makes of it the first two chapters of his book.[19] However, my selection of the theme of self-knowledge and God-knowledge was originally inspired by Martin Luther's insight into Bernard's insights. In Luther's second lectures on the Psalms (*Operationes*) of the early 1520s, we find his direct reliance on Saint Bernard: 'For just as, according to Bernard, knowledge of self without the knowledge of God leads to despair, so knowledge of God without the knowledge of self leads to presumption.'[20] In his lectures on the *First Letter of John* in 1527, Luther returns to these insights,[21] and again in 1532 in his lecture on *Psalm 51*:

> The knowledge of God and of man is divine and true theological wisdom. And it is knowledge of God and man in this way, that it actually refers itself to the God who justifies, and to the man who is a sinner. Consequently, the actual object of theology is man, who-is guilty and corrupt, and God, who justifies and is Savior.[22]

In both these later instances (1527 and 1532), Luther did not mention Bernard by name, as by then he appears to have completely appropriated Bernard's theological insights.

As any God-seeker knows, the God-issue is reflected and mirrored in spiritual writings. And Bernard is one of the best examples of this. Especially in the last two of his formal writings, Bernard wrote of God and of man's relationship to God. These two major works are his 'five books' *On Consideration* and the last of the *Sermons on the Song of Songs*.[23] A few selections will be presented from these works. The

God-issue, however, is ever present in all of Bernard's writings; as the selection of texts shows, the majority of them taken from his sermons rather than his treatises. A major, perhaps even the most dominating topic in Bernard's works is the inter-relationship of God-knowledge and self-knowledge: recognizing oneself as a sinner and God as one's savior. To know God, a person must know himself or herself, which is the fundamental principle of Bernard's spirituality and theology. He learned this principle from the ancient oracle of Delphi at which he hints in *Sermon 23 on the Canticle* and *Sermon 40 on Diverse Subjects*; he also learned it from Augustine's prayer, 'O unchanging God, let me know myself; let me know you,'[24] to which he refers in his *Sermon 2 on Diverse Subjects*. Bernard is rooted in the best of patristic spirituality and theology.[25] This twofold knowledge turns out to be Bernard's central pastoral concern, and in explicating that concern he shows himself a genius at shepherding.[26] At the same time, Bernard knows that a certain curiosity is the first step toward the sin of pride, the curiosity through which Satan fell.[27] The issue of the knowledge of self was dominant in the twelfth century. Peter Abelard, Bernard's opponent, wrote a book on it, *Scito teipsum*, which is simultaneously a book on ethics.[28]

Any introduction to Bernard and his writings requires a brief sketch of his life. However, that is easier said than done because he was a 'difficult saint,'[29] 'not easy to read,'[30] and our knowledge of him seems to be based on legends from the *First Life of Bernard* (*Vita prima*),[31] a hagiographic account by William of Saint Thierry[32] who knew Bernard after he had become an abbot at Clairvaux. William's fundamental assertion is that Bernard was a holy man, conserving objective data for the use of future historians was not his concern.[33] As important as the *First Life* may be the *Clairvaux Saint Bernard Office*[34] is another hagiographic source. In this text, Bernard is called a 'shepherd of God's people,'[35] a title which actually sums up quite well his life and work. The best way, however, of gaining authentic insights into Bernard is to let him speak to us through his own words. An anthology is a good place to start.

Perhaps critically distancing himself from certain opinions or rumors about him which circulated during his life time, Bernard felt compelled to write: 'I am not what you think or say I am.'[36] Toward the end of

# Introduction

his life, he wrote of himself in a letter dated about 1150, revealing just a little bit of his own knowledge of himself, but not too much:

> It is time for me not to be forgetful of myself. My monstrous life, my plagued conscience, calls out to you. For I am the chimera of my age, neither cleric nor layman. I have long ago abandoned the monastic life, but have kept the habit of a monk. I do not wish to write you what, I dare say, you have [already] heard from others: what I am doing, what are my purposes, through what dangers I pass in the world, or rather down what precipices I am hurled.[37]

The reader interested in details of Bernard' biography would do well to read his other letters, 551 altogether, which mirror Bernard's relationships and pastoral, spiritual, and personal concerns.[38]

Born of a noble family at Fontaines near Dijon, France, in 1090 (or 1091?), he was schooled from 1098 to 1108 at the splendid school of Saint-Vorles at Châtillon. This schooling included the reading of Latin classics: Virgil, Terence, Ovid, and also Boëthius. Bernard lost his mother when he was thirteen years of age. He was supposed to enter the career of a cleric, while his brothers were meant to pursue a career in the military. After Bernard entered the cloister in 1113, his uncle, Villain d'Aigremont, the later bishop of Langres (1125-1136) tried to dissuade him, as Bernard's *Letter* 2, from about 1120, indicates.

Bernard convinced thirty of his relatives and friends to join him at Cîteaux as monks. This monastery thus became a place of and for his own kinfolk,[39] a cloister of his clan. The same is true of the new monastic foundation at Clairvaux, of which Bernard became the founding abbot in 1115. The area around Clairvaux had been used for many years as a den of thieves. Bernard and his monks turned it into sacred space, according to William's account (Chapter V of the *Vita prima*).[40] Although not the oldest of his brothers, Bernard appears to have become a *pater familias*, as head of the monastic household of Clairvaux.

Was Bernard ordained to the priesthood? Can one simply assume that Bernard was ordained in 1115 when Bishop William of Champeaux confirmed him as abbot of Clairvaux? In the history of pastoral care, it is not clearly demonstrable that all abbots should be priests or deacons.[41] That same history shows that one must differentiate between 'pastor,' 'priest,' and 'monk' because originally the monastic Orders were Orders of lay people. One may not automatically assume that all monks were priests. On the issue of Bernard's ordination, the *Vita prima*, Chapter VII, reports as follows:

> Newly arrived at Clairvaux, Bernard needed ordination to the ministry for which he had been enlisted. The see of Langres, however, to which it belonged to ordain him, happened to be vacant, and so the brethren were inquiring about where they should take him for the rite. The good name of the near by and venerable bishop of Châlons-sur-Marne, the highly reputed Master William of Champeaux soon presented itself. And so it was decided that they should send Bernard to him.[42]

Did William ordain him to the priesthood first and then consecrate him as abbot? Or was Bernard consecrated abbot without ordination to the priesthood? Or must one presuppose his ordination to the priesthood at an earlier date in Cîteaux? We do not really know. The so-called *First Life* of Bernard does not mention any ordination to the priesthood. Not even when he became abbot in 1115 was any note made that he was ordained to the priesthood. However, one may not necessarily conclude that he was not ordained. William's Chapter V simply reads: 'Just as they were leaving, Dom Stephen took the further step of appointing Bernard himself as their abbot.' In the case of a new foundation, the first superior is appointed, not elected.

However, it was very important to his hagiographer to show, in the same Chapter V, that Abbot Bernard was concerned about the salvation of souls, that he was a 'pastor'.[43] We read that Bernard's 'great concern has ever been rather the salvation of the many' and 'his only consolation being the salvation of many'. In Chapter VI, William makes the observation that 'Bernard's men took care not to lay on his mind the burden of concern for outward affairs'. They wanted him to have only 'concern for their souls,' that is, be their spiritual advisor. However, when Bernard gave them sermons on spiritual matters, they scarcely caught 'what he was saying,' according to William. Perhaps his sermonizing was all too spiritual a preaching for many of them. Politely, his men 'treated with reverence even the parts they did not comprehend.' 'All his preaching would be more of a stumbling block to them than a source of edification.' The same lack of real understanding occurred especially when Bernard 'heard them, one by one, confessing to him and accusing themselves of the various illusory thoughts common to humanity.' In VI, 28, we even learn of Bernard preaching a 'hard sermon'. Nevertheless, Bernard became a 'fisherman in God's hand,' as the hagiographer calls him, that is, a spiritual director and pastor who leads souls to God:

> Preaching was so powerful a force with him, and he shone so brilliantly at softening hard hearts among his hearers, that scarcely ever did he come home void of conversions. By and by, as he grew more skillful in speaking the Word of God..., he became rather like a net, or, rather, quite a fisherman in the hand of God.[44]

It is no wonder, then, that during Bernard's lifetime, about 700 monks lived at Clairvaux. Bernard relied on their assistance as secretaries, councilmen, administrators, and even economic advisors.[45] The Abbey of Clairvaux would give birth to sixty-seven daughter houses. They were usually built in valleys (as Clair-vaux itself) or near water sources,[46] not on mountains as was the case with many Benedictine monasteries (like Monte Cassino, for example). A further contrast with the Benedictines was the Cistercian undyed cowl in place of Benedictine black.[47]

Bernard died in 1153. A story about Bernard on his sickbed, even though a legend, captures quite well his thoughts on death and Judgment Day:

> There was a time when the man of God fell so seriously ill that he seemed about to breathe his last. He was rapt in ecstasy and saw himself being presented before God's judgment seat, while Satan stood opposite him and peppered him with malicious charges.... Unperturbed, [Bernard] said: 'I admit I am unworthy, and unable by merits of my own to gain entrance to the kingdom of heaven. On the other hand, my Lord has won the kingdom by a twofold right, namely, by inheritance from his Father and by the merits of his passion. The first he has reserved for himself but the second he gives to me.[48]

Fig. 2 Medulla, Baudeloo, 1653

Fig. 3 Freschoz, Hauterieve, c. 1660

Fig. 4 Johann Heiss, Leitheim, 1696

Fig. 5 School of Altomonte, Wilhering, c. 1760

# Introduction

This story may have had its origin in a text of the genuine works of Bernard, in the *Sermon on the Seven Gifts of the Holy Spirit*.[49] This sermon speaks of Christ according to his divinity, Christ being co-eternal and equal in everything with the Father. Christ did not need his suffering on the cross to earn the kingdom of heaven for himself. He already had his own right to the kingdom as God's Son. However, Christ, by the price of his sacrifice, obtained the right to the kingdom for others and decided to share it with others.

The image of Bernard the fisherman of souls and pastor portrays the essence of Bernard's life and work. Yet, there always has been, as it were, 'several Bernards'.[50] His image in the history of art is largely determined by legend. Artistic depictions show him with the devil, with the Virgin Mary (often as *Lactatio Bernardi*, that is, Mary squirting mother's milk on Bernard's lips), and with the Crucified who takes his arm off the crossbeam to embrace him (*Amplexus Bernardi*).[51] Bernard's image may also be shaped by Pseudo-Bernardine texts such as the *Vita Christi*, which includes a text on the 'embrace' which goes: 'See, his head is bent to kiss, his arms are outstretched to embrace.'[52]

A summary of Bernard's life was provided for the anniversary of Bernard's birth in 1990 through images on an embroidered wall hanging by Sr. Dr. Mechthild Bernart (now abbess). The outer circle of images that surround the inner circle with the Crucified embracing Bernard (see depiction at the end of the book) show his birthplace at Fontaines with the birth date, 1090, his entry at Cîteaux, the founding of Clairvaux, the edification at Clairvaux, Bernard in meditation, Bernard the healer, the miracle worker, Bernard and Pope Innocent, Bernard and the conversion of King Roger of Sicily, Bernard and William of Aquitaine, Bernard and Peter Abelard making peace, Bernard as preacher of the crusade, and at the conclusion of the circle we see, as a symbol of the continuation of Bernard's work, the outline of the church tower of the nunnery of Thyrnau with the year 1990.[53]

In scholarly writings on the history of spirituality, the image of Bernard the mystic appears to dominate. With Étienne Gilson's work in the 1930s on the 'mystical theology' of Bernard, not only his mysticism, but also his theology came to the fore, as Gilson placed the term 'theology' into the title of his book: *La théologie mystique de saint Bernard*.[54] A reprint in English appeared for the Bernard Year

1990 when his 900th birthday was celebrated.[55] His mysticism was also explored by Michael Casey in his *Bernard of Clairvaux: Man, Monk, Mystic*.[56]

For some time the notions 'mystical theology' and 'monastic theology' competed for recognition in the effort to characterize Bernard's theology.[57] For centuries the title 'theologian' was denied him. However, that Bernard was a true 'theologian' is no longer disputed today. Based on the view of 'Bernard the theologian,' another aspect, which has rarely come into focus, may surface now: Bernard the 'pastor'. Bernard was a pastor with 'charisma,' as Jean Leclercq has written in his contribution to the nonacentenary celebration in 1990.[58] Bernard was one of the most pastoral leaders that the Church has ever seen. This is so even though the primary purpose of his own Cistercian Order was not to provide pastoral care in parishes or train monks for pastoral ministries, as monks are not called to preach in public.[59] The history of pastoral care reflects a reluctance of the contemplative Orders to become involved in general pastoral care outside the monastic circle.[60] Bernard seems to be an exception with his pastoral care outside of the monastery.

*The Rule of Saint Benedict* does not mention anything on pastoral care by monks for outsiders.[61] Preaching, baptizing, hearing the confession of outsiders, and the administration of parishes was not a monk's task. A synod at Rouen in 1074 decided that no monk is to be in charge of a parish.[62] The Cistercians, according to their *Consuetudines* of 1134, were not to hear the confession of, or give communion to, outsiders or to bury them. The General Chapter of 1157 prohibited abbots or monks from baptizing except in near death situations when no parish priest was available.[63] Nevertheless, from the evidence of his works, Bernard ordained to the priesthood or not, still needs to be given a place of honor in the history of pastoral care and 'pastoral theology'.[64] The Bernard image of the historians[65] must incorporate Bernard the master theologian and the pastor of souls: From Master to Pastor. Bernard was more a spiritual director of souls than an instructor in doctrine. This does not mean, however, that the texts of this pastor become easier to read. He is far from being a simple, pious author of edifying tracts with little substance. Nor does this mean that Pastor Bernard's sermons are improvisations. Whatever of his sermons his monks recorded, he himself carefully rewrote for publication.66

Bernard's own primary concern was that bishops and abbots should be shepherds of souls.67 His long *Letter* 42 was intended for bishops; it was a response to a request made by the archbishop of Sens in 1127 or 1128,68 asking him for an opinion on the nature of the office of a bishop. Bernard's response is known as *On the Conduct and Duties of Bishops*. The introductory paragraphs of the treatise are inspired by the biblical metaphor for 'the ministry' of the good shepherd as found especially in John 21:15-17.69 Bernard repeatedly wrote of the duty of 'pastoral care' of a bishop, and warned not to exercise dominion but ministry.70 For priests (clerics), Bernard wrote his sermon *On Conversion*, which may be understood as a treatise on the spirituality of priests.71

Bernard was more a universal and monastic 'pastor' than an academic teacher, even though he did lecture to the students of Paris. He did this not for the purpose of teaching doctrine as to convert them to the spiritual life. The historical Bernard was not primarily interested in dogmatic questions, or in hunting heretics. He needed to be dragged into the famed doctrinal controversy with Peter Abelard.72 Entering the controversy was motivated, he says, by his pastoral concern for the faith of the common folk. He charged Abelard of pastoral carelessness, calling him a 'prelate without care'.73

Bernard's ideas on pastoral care and pastoral responsibility are expressed with the Latin *solicitudo*, taken from his favorite biblical author, Saint Paul, 2 Cor 11:28, *solicitudo omnium Ecclesiarum*, which Bernard quoted in Book Two of *On Consideration*,74 writing about the title 'bishop' as referring not to dominion, but to pastoral care as the duty and responsibility of bishops.75 Pastoral care, however, did not mean to him disregarding catholicity for the sake of being 'pastoral'. Bernard advocates a return to 'catholic unity'.76 The Church is the *Catholica*, a notion which he uses both as an adjective and as a substantive.77 He may also say that there is catholic truth, *catholica veritas*.78

Bernard had a gift of powerful preaching, which is one of the reasons why his sermons were collected and widely disseminated. It seems that his sermons were rated as highly as those of the Church Fathers. Since Saint Benedict's Rule provided for the public reading of texts from the orthodox and catholic fathers (Rule of Saint Benedict 9), Bernard's sermons were later in monasteries used like patristic homilies as liturgical readings.[79]

Bernard scholars have concentrated for the past fifty years (necessarily and rightly so) on Bernard the Philosopher,[80] 'Bernard the Theologian,'[81] 'Bernardus Magister,'[82] or on the 'essential Bernard,' by featuring the dogmatic, monastic, and mystic theologian and statesman.[83] True, Bernard, a multi-faceted personality, was all these and more. He was an eminent pastor and a mentor of pastors in their tasks of pastoral or spiritual care. Bernard did not use the term *theologia* as did Peter Abelard. Bernard did not understand himself so much as a theologian in the contemporaneous sense of the word, but perhaps more as a Christian philosopher in the Augustinian sense, and most of all as a student of the salvific and sacred Scriptures.[84] His notion 'philosophy' is completely Christocentric as he declares that his only philosophy is to know Jesus and him Crucified, quoting Saint Paul: 'This is my philosophy,... to know Jesus and him crucified' [1 Cor 2:2].[85] Again he says: 'It is enough for me; I desire to know nothing more than Jesus and him crucified' [1 Cor 2:2].[86] The 'philosophy of Paul' is far superior to any other philosophy of the world.[87] The 'teachers of the world' do not know the salvific science which only the 'disciples of Christ' attain in Jesus as the Crucified [1 Cor 2:2].[88]

Bernard is a pastor through and through. His view of any ecclesiastical office is governed by the biblical metaphor of the pastor.[89] This metaphor is placed at the center of his reflections on the Church.[90] All his thinking appears to be put to the service of sermonizing, teaching, preaching, and spiritual direction. In his pastoral care, preaching ranked very high. However, it was a preaching by a person who is more like a bowl than a pipe (to use this image from Bernard's SC 18.3)l: 'If you are wise, you will show yourself more like a reservoir than a canal.'[91] And Bernard's observation sounds like a statement describing the present-day situation: 'Today there are many in the Church who act like canals, the reservoirs are far too rare.'[92] This phrase demonstrates how deeply concerned Bernard was about good pastoral care, based on solid theology. Denis Farkasfalvy has summarized the emerging image of Bernard as a pastoral theologian in this way:

> Bernard's approach to theology is classical and evenly open in all directions. But it is equally true that Bernard sees himself as a theologian always in the context of being an abbot, a teacher, a churchman and a preacher. His role as a theologian is always focused on teaching people about themselves, leading them to the discovery of the human plight in themselves, guiding them to conversion and so to connect their human experience with an experience of Christ.[93]

This new image of Bernard has emerged also in Gerhard B. Winkler's 1993 study of Bernard's letters as means of pastoral care,[94] and in G. R. Evans' Bernard biography of 2000, in the series of 'Great Medieval Thinkers,' where, however, Bernard's pastoral concerns are treated within the chapter on 'Political Theology'.[95]

Bernard's work as a 'pastor' was grounded in his biblical scholarship. Bernard's interpretations of the Bible earned him the title *Doctor mellifluus*, 'honey-sweet teacher,' that is, for his ability to make the Word of God flow like honey. This honorific title was used for the first time in the 1508 edition of his works. It is an expression of a great appreciation for Bernard's eloquent spiritual preaching.[96] The adjective *mellifluus* is probably inspired by the Latin version of Joel 3:18, which is quoted in his Marian homily on Luke 1 (Miss 1.1). Bernard used the verse for his characterization of the evangelist's way with words, writing of his 'mellifluous language'.[97] This verse, Joel 3:18, was quoted also by Peter the Venerable, but in reference to Bernard's own impressive way with words.[98] A contemporary observer, Bishop Anselm of Havelberg, a Premonstratensian, wrote this in 1149 on Bernard's captivating interpretation of the Bible:

> When I visited the Church of Rome, I saw and heard the abbot of Clairvaux .... In the midst of clerics seated around him he was, at the command of Pope Innocent interpreting and clarifying the words of the Holy Scriptures.[99]

The prince of the Renaissance humanists, Desiderius Erasmus of Rotterdam, was keenly aware of Bernard's 'elegant' sermonizing. He believed Bernard's *Sermons on the Canticle* belonged to the top ten on the bestseller list.[100] Our text selections want to help to return Bernard to a top spot on a present-day bestseller list of spiritual writings.

Bernard the pastor and theologian understood the Bible as the 'Word of salvation,'[101] and he obviously adhered to his own 'Scripture principle' when he declared: 'I follow the authority of the divine books' and the 'testimony of the Scriptures'.[102] On interpreting the Word of God, he writes:

> In the exposition of the holy and mystical words, let us proceed in a cautious and simple way, let us display the way of the Scripture which speaks with our words of the wisdom which is hidden in the mystery; while [Scripture] expresses itself figuratively, it insinuates God into our affections.[103]

Bernard's advice to carefully interpret the sacred texts rests on the assumption that there are several meanings of a given text. No one in his day assumed that a given Bible verse had only one meaning.[104] Furthermore, to Bernard the Bible was the living Word that speaks to the soul. The 'words of the Word,' Christ, are directed to the soul.[105] Bernard declared himself a 'minister of Christ' and 'administrator of the mysteries of God' with words from 1 Cor 4:1-4.[106] The good pastor always carries in his purse the Word of God.

Bernard himself was nurtured by the Scriptures on which he meditated in 'sacred reading,' that is, in a process of assimilating the Word of God and letting its meaning spread into his entire being, 'a process of impregnation, interiorization, personalization of the word of God.[107] 'Sacred reading' is simply the praying over Scripture in preference to any other spiritual text. It is a conscientious effort to make the word and Word of God central to one's life.[108] About this monastic practice, Charles Cummings wrote: 'Our monastic predecessors in past centuries lived by God's word, thought in its categories, spoke in its language and wrote as if they had a biblical concordance connected to their pen. These were fruits of a lifetime of sacred reading.'[109] M. Basil Pennington called this 'sacred reading' a meeting with God in and through his Word'.[110] Thus, Scripture study was not an academic exercise for Bernard. He was not seeking the 'letter' but the 'spirit'.[111]

In Bernard's high appreciation of the word and the Word of God in Scripture, one may see a resemblance to the sixteenth-century reformers and their 'Theology of the Word' and 'Scripture principle'. Luther was a representative of monastic theology and 'sacred reading' insofar as his concept of a theology of the Word of God was similarly and essentially connected to the interweaving of sacred reading, prayer, mediation, and life experience.[112] Luther may have been a mystic of the Word.[113] He understood the Word of God primarily as a 'living voice' (*viva vox*) speaking to us, not so much a book.[114] Even in the lecture hall he used what one may call an 'orational approach,' a prayerful approach, to Scripture interpretation.[115]

However, the monastic scholars of the school of Saint Bernard and their 'Scripture principle' did not view Scripture in terms of either/or, that is 'either' scripture 'or' tradition, but coupled their 'Scripture principle' with the 'Fathers Principle' that is, with a concern to be in agreement with the Church Fathers.[116] Bernard occasionally appealed to their authority.[117] To adhere to the 'Scripture principle' was laborious for Bernard. Studying the Bible for preaching alone, but with the individual listener's needs in mind, was no small effort for him when he had to 'draw waters from the open streams of the Scriptures and provide for the needs' of each of his monks. 'The divine word is a water of the wisdom that saves.'[118] He wished that this type of spiritual care would be provided by others, not himself.[119] Nevertheless, he remained a curate of souls, as his 'Scripture principle' was a pastoral principle. Even his *Praise of the New Knighthood* was a work motivated by pastoral care as it provides a spiritual tour of the places about which the Scriptures speak.[120]

As the works of Saint Bernard continue to be studied, a new image of Bernard is emerging which secures him a place of honor not only in the history of spirituality and theology, but also in the history of the Christian pastoral care and shepherding of souls. Bernard is the outstanding universal pastor, with a definite threefold concept of pastoral care, fashioned from the matrix of John 21:17, Christ's triple questioning of Peter and mandating him to feed his fold. Bernard explained Christ's triple mandate for pastors in this way: (1) to live an exemplary life, (2) to teach, and (3) to pray.[121]

Christ incarnate and crucified is at the heart of Bernard's knowledge of God and of self, as he reflects on the Son of God who was sent to save sinners. A distinctive feature of his philosophy and theology is the inseparable connection of knowledge of God and of self. And so the two-fold knowledge, that is, knowledge of God as giver, and knowledge of self as receiver, has become the leitmotif of this selection of spiritual texts, which, I hope, will invite further reading.

Our starting point for this anthology is the subject of the knowledge of self in the way Bernard perceived this task which he inherited from Greek antiquity as he himself confirms (Chapter 1). He insists on our knowing ourselves as sinners before God the savior. Knowledge is twofold: knowledge of self is intrinsically connected to knowledge of God. Knowledge of self includes the awareness of man being Christ's beast of burden (Chapter 2), and the awareness of what troubles us (Chapter 3). Help is found in knowing the Word of God in sacred reading as an encounter with God and with Christ, the Word of God (Chapter 4). Bernard wants us to attend the school of the triune God (Chapter 5). There we shall learn true godliness and worship of God (Chapter 6); we learn that it is 'hard to be humble' as the lyrics of a contemporary country song has it. However, Bernard teaches us that it is very smart to be humble before God (Chapter 7). We come to know God in Christ the savior (Chapter 8), so that our only philosophy would be – speaking with St. Paul - to know Christ and him Crucified (Chapter 9). Having gained this insight, we will understand that the accusation of self before God is necessary and corresponds with the justification of the sinner by God (Chapter 10). Then, we shall realize that it is enough to know that our merits are not enough to save us (Chapter 11). Finally we learn what Bernard means by pastoral care of souls (Chapter 12) and that we need to know the spiritual direction that we take, and to observe our spiritual progress from faith toward understanding (Chapter 13).

The text selections are meant as an introduction to Bernard's philosophy, theology, spirituality, and pastoral care. He surely still has something to tell us today as he remains a classic of western spirituality and a great Christian thinker.

# Notes

1. See Bernardo Olivera, 'Help in Reading St. Bernard,' *Word & Spirit: A Monastic Review* 12 (1990) 3-20, here 9.
2. See John R. Sommerfeldt, *The Spiritual Teachings of Bernard of Clairvaux* (Kalamazoo: Cistercian Publications, 1991).
3. On such scholarship, see David C. Steinmetz, 'The Superiority of Pre-Critical Exegesis,' *Theology Today* 27 (1980) 27-38; Richard A. Muller and John L. Thomson, 'The Significance of Precritical Exegesis: Retrospect and Prospect,' in Richard A. Muller and John L. Thomson, eds., *Biblical Interpretation in the Era of the Reformation: Essays Presented to David C. Steinmetz in Honor of His Sixtieth Birthday* (Grand Rapids: Eerdmans, 1996) 335-45.
4. See Jean Leclercq, *Maurice Blondel lecteur de Bernard de Clairvaux* (Brussels: Lessius, 2001).
5. M. Basil Pennington, *Bernard of Clairvaux: A Lover Teaching the Way of Love. Selected Spiritual Writings* (Hyde Park, NY: New City Press, 1997) 8-9.
6. Olivera, 9. On Bernard's education, see G. R. Evans, 'The Classical Education of Bernard of Clairvaux,' *Cîteaux* 33 (1982) 121-34.
7. As to the dates for his sermons, I rely on the various introductions in the German/Latin edition by Gerhard B. Winkler, *Bernhard von Clairvaux: Sämtliche Werke* (Innsbruck: Tyrolia, 1990-1999). English translations based on the critical edition of these sermons are just now forthcoming from Cistercian Publications, such as *Advent and Christmas Sermons* (Cistercian Fathers 51), and *Occasional Sermons* (Cistercian Fathers 68).
8. Gerhard B. Winkler, *Bernhard von Clairvaux: Die eine umfassende Kirche—Einheit in der Vielfalt* (Innsbruck: Tyrolia, 2001) 150; from here on quoted as Winkler, *Bernhard*.
9. See G. R. Evans, *Bernard of Clairvaux* (New York and Oxford: Oxford University Press, 2000) in the series 'Great Medieval Thinkers'; hereafter quoted as Evans.
10. See Adriaan H. Bredero, *Bernard of Clairvaux Between Cult and History* (Grand Rapids: Eerdmans, 1996) 4, with reference to Leclercq's studies; hereafter quoted as Bredero; see also Olivera, 8; Evans, 19.
11. See Jean Leclercq, *Bernard of Clairvaux and the Cistercian Spirit*, trans. Claire Lavoie (Kalamazoo: Cistercian Publications, 1976) 9.
12. See Jean Leclercq, 'Der heilige Bernhard und Deutschland,' in Dieter R. Bauer and Gotthard Fuchs, eds., *Bernhard von Clairvaux und der Beginn der Moderne* (Innsbruck and Vienna: Tyrolia, 1996) 321-25.
13. See Theo Bell, *Honing uit de rots: Teksten van Bernard van Clairvaux* (Zoetermeer: Uitgeverij Meinema, 2001).

14 See *Bernard of Clairvaux: Selected Works*. Translation and Foreword by G. R. Evans, Introduction by Jean Leclercq; preface by Ewert H. Cousins (New York, Mahwah: Paulist Press, 1987).

15 See Paul Diemer, *Love Without Measure: Extracts from the Writings of St Bernard of Clairvaux* (Kalamazoo: Cistercian Publications, 1990); M. Basil Pennington, *Bernard of Clairvaux: A Lover Teaching the Way of Love* (Hyde Park, NY: New City Press, 1997); Edith Scholl, ed., *In the School of Love: An Anthology of Early Cistercian Texts* (Kalamazoo: Cistercian Publications, 2000).

16 See Olivera, 4-6.

17 In the Western tradition, the topic of self-knowledge becomes prominent with Augustine; see Edward Booth, 'St. Augustine and the Western Tradition of Self-Knowing,' *The Saint Augustine Lecture 1986* (Villanova: University Press, 1989). Contemporary philosophy does not seem to go beyond self-knowledge; see Brie Gertler, ed., *Privileged Access: Philosophical Accounts of Self-Knowledge* (Aldershot, UK: Ashgate, 2003).

18 See Leclercq, *Bernard of Clairvaux and the Cistercian Spirit*, 129-30.

19 See T.H.L. Parker, *John Calvin: A Biography* (Philadelphia: The Westminster Press, 1975) 73.

20 See Franz Posset, *Pater Bernhardus: Martin Luther and Bernard of Clairvaux*. Foreword by Michael Casey, Preface by + Bernhard Lohse (Kalamazoo: Cistercian Publications, 1999) 225-26, hereafter quoted as *Pater Bernhardus*; Theo Bell, *Divus Bernhardus. Bernhard von Clairvaux in Martin Luthers Schriften* (Mainz: Verlag Philipp von Zabern, 1993) 115-16.

21 See Posset, *Pater Bernhardus*, 226.

22 Quoted in Helmar Junghans, 'Die Mitte der Theologie Luthers,' *Die Zeichen der Zeit* 37 (1983) 190-94, repinted in Helmar Junghans, *Spätmittelalter, Luthers Reformation, Kirche in Sachsen: Ausgewählte Aufsätze*, eds. Michael Beyer and Günther Wartenberg (Leipzig: Evangelische Verlagsanstalt, 2001) 91-98, here 92. English translation by Gerard S. Krispin, 'The Center of the Theology of Martin Luther,' in Jon D. Vieker, ed., *And Every Tongue Confess: Essays in Honor of Norman Nagel on the Occasion of His Sixty-fifth Birthday* (Dearborn, MI: The Nagel Festschrift Committee, 1990) 179-94; see also *Luther Digest* 1 (1993) 97-98. In the critical edition of Luther's works, the *Weimarer Ausgabe* (=WA), see vol. 40-II:327, line 11 - 328, line 2.

23 See M. Basil Pennington and Yael Katzir, *Bernard of Clairvaux: A Saint's Life in Word and Image* (Huntington, IN: Our Sunday Visitor Publishing Company, 1994) 251-52.

24 *Soliloquies* 2.1.1; Donald X. Burt, "*Let Me Know Myself...*" *Reflections on the Prayer of Augustine* (Collegeville: Liturgical Press, 2002).
25 (Including Origen), see James W. Zona, "Set Love in Order in Me': Eros-Knowing in Origen and Desiderium-Knowing in Saint Bernard,' *Cistercian Studies Quarterly* 34 (1999) 157-82.
26 See Denis Farkasfalvy, "La conoscenza di Dio nel pensiero di san Bernardo,' *Studi su s. Bernardo di Chiaravalle nell'ottavo centenario della canonizzazione: Convegno Internazionale, Certosa di Firenze: 6-9 Novembre 1974* (Rome: Editiones Cistercienses, 1975) 201-214. Winkler, *Bernhard*, 154.
27 On *curiositas*, see *On the Steps of Humility and Pride* 10.28, SBOp 3:38. On Satan's curiosity, ibid. 9.25, SBOp 3:35 and 10.38, SBOp 3:45. See ƒtienne Gilson, *The Mystical Theology of Saint Bernard*, trans. A H.C. Downes (New York: Sheed and Ward, 1940; Kalamazoo: Cistercian Publications, reprint 1990) Appendix I: *Curiositas*, 155-57; G. R. Evans, 'What We Are Not Supposed To Know,' in E. Rozanne Elder, ed., *The Joy of Learning and the Love of God: Studies in Honor of Jean Leclercq* (Kalamazoo: Cistercian Publications, 1995) 309-326, here 319.
28 The full title reads *Ethica seu scito teipsum*, *Patrologia Latina* 178:633-78.
29 See Brian P. McGuire, *A Difficult Saint: Bernard of Clairvaux and His Tradition* (Kalamazoo: Cistercian Publications, 1991).
30 Olivera, 9.
31 All the English quotations from *Vita prima* depend on or are directly taken from the Guadalupe Translations by Martinus Cawley, *Bernard of Clairvaux. Early Biographies, Volume I by William of St. Thierry* (Lafayette, Oregon, 1990); hereafter quoted as Cawley.
32 On this issue, see Adriaan H. Bredero, "Der Beitrag Wilhelms von Saint-Theirry zur Heiligsprechung Bernhards von Clairvaux und der biographische Wert seines kultbezogenen Textes aus historischer Sicht," in: *Vita Religiosa im Mittelalter. Festschrift für Kaspar Elm zum 70. Geburtstag* (Berliner Historische Studien 31 = Ordensstudien 13), ed. Franz J. Felten et al. (Berlin: Duncker & Humblot, 1999) 169-82.
33 See Michael Casey, 'Toward a Methodology for the Vita Prima: Translating the First Life into Biography,' in *Bernardus Magister: Papers Presented at the Nonacentenary Celebration of the Birth of Saint Bernard of Clairvaux, Kalamazoo, Michigan* (1990), ed. John R. Sommerfeldt (Kalamazoo: Cistercian Publications, 1992) 55-70, here 57; Casey, 'Bernard of Clairvaux: The Face Behind the Persona,' *Cistercian Studies Quarterly* 27 (1992) 133-51. Ulrich K pf, 'Probleme einer Biographie Bernhards von Clair-

vaux: Bemerkungen zu Peter Dinzelbachers Bernhard-Buch,' *Zeitschrift für Württembergische Landesgeschichte* 59 (2000) 413-26.

34 See Chrysogonus Waddell, 'The Clairvaux Saint Bernard Office: Ikon of a Saint,' in: *Bernardus Magister*, 381-421.

35 *Pastor populi dei*, Waddell 393.

36 *Non sum talis qualis putor vel dicor*, Ep 11.10, SBOp 7:60,22; see Jean Leclercq, 'Toward a Sociological Interpretation of the Various Saint Bernards,' in *Bernardus Magister*, 27.

37 Ep 250.4 to Prior Bernard of the Carthusian monastery at Portes, SBOp 8:147, lines 1-5; for the date, see the notes to Ep 250 in the German/Latin edition, 3:1123; Bredero 188; see also the book title of E. Rozanne Elder and John R. Sommerfeldt, eds., *The Chimaera of his Age: Studies on Bernard of Clairvaux* (Kalamazoo: Cistercian Publications, 1980).

38 See *The Letters of Saint Bernard of Clairvaux*, translated by Bruno Scott James (Kalamazoo: Cistercian Publications, 1998; reprint of the 1953 edition). Recent biographies include the following; Jean Leclercq, *Bernard de Clairvaux* (Paris and Tournai: Desclée, 1989); German edition: *Bernhard von Clairvaux: Ein Mann prägt seine Zeit* (Munich 1990); Italian edition: *Bernardo di Chiaravalle* (Milan: Vita e Pensiero, 1992). Peter Dinzelbacher, *Bernhard von Clairvaux: Leben und Werk des berühmten Zisterziensers* (Darmstadt: Primus Verlag 1998). M. Kilian Hufgard, *Bernard of Clairvaux's Broad Impact on Medieval Culture* (Lewiston, N.Y.: E. Mellen Press, 2001).

39 In German, *Sippenkloster* or *Familienkloster*; see Winkler, *Bernhard*, 22-23.

40 See Cawley, 34.

41 See Philipp Hofmeister, 'Mönchtum und Seelsorge bis zum 13. Jahrhundert,' *Studien und Mitteilungen zur Geschichte des Benediktiner-Ordens und seiner Zweige* 65 (1955) 209-73.

42 Cawley, 42.

43 The French *curé* is derived from Latin *cura* (care); the German *Seelsorger* literally means a 'person caring for souls.'

44 *Vita prima*, 7; see Cawley, 75. See Anselme Dimier, *Saint Bernard 'pêcheur de Dieu'* (Paris: 1953).

45 See Gerhard B. Winkler, Introduction, in: *Bernhard von Clairvaux: Sämtliche Werke*, 1:16.

46 The names of numerous foundations in German speaking lands reveal this preference, as many names of these monasteries end with *-t[h]al* (valley), *-[b]ach* (creek), or *-bronn* (water well) as, for instance, in Gnadenthal, Lichtenthal, Seligenthal, Wonnental, Heilsbronn, Maulbronn, Aldersbach, Bronnbach, Ebersbach, Eschenbach, Heisterbach, Raitenhaslach, Schlierbach, Wurmsbach.

47 See Winkler, *Sämtliche Werke*, 1:21.
48 Based on *Vita prima* I,12,57; Cawley, 70. The translation given here is that of *The Golden Legend: Readings on the Saints*, trans. William Granger Ryan (Princeton: Princeton University Press, 1993) 2 volumes, here 2:102f. See Posset, *Pater Bernhardus*, 297-304.
49 Sermo varius: De septem donis Spiritus sancti, 2; SBOp 6/I,46,10-14. Another source might be SC 61.5; see Posset, 'The "Double Right to Heaven": Saint Bernard's Impact in the Sixteenth Century,' *Cistercian Studies Quarterly* 38 (2003), 263-273..
51 See Jean-Claude Schmitt, 'Saint Bernard et son image,' *Colloque de Lyon-Cîteaux-Dijon: Bernard de Clairvaux: Histoire, Mentalités, Spiritualité* (Paris: Cerf, 1992) 639-57, here 651. Franz Posset, 'Saint Bernard of Clairvaux in the Devotion Theology, and Art of the Sixteenth Century,' *Lutheran Quarterly* 11 (1997) 308-352, with depictions of Bernard and the devil and the *Lactatio Bernardi*. Franz Posset, 'The Crucified Embraces Saint Bernard: The Beginnings of the *Amplexus Bernardi*,'' *Cistercian Studies Quarterly* 33 (1998) 289-314, with depictions from the fourteenth and fifteenth centuries. James France, *The Cistercians in Medieval Art* (Kalamazoo: Cistercian Publications, 1998) 26-49.
52 *Vita Christi* II, 64, 677b, as quoted in Leo Scheffczyk ed., *Faith in Christ and the Worship of Christ*, trans. Graham Harrison (San Francisco: Ignatius Press, 1986) 87-88.
53 As explained by the artist in *Bernhard von Clairvaux* (St. Ottilien: EOS Druckerei, 1990) 9.
54 First edition: 1939.
55 See Gilson (1940, 1990). See also Joseph Lortz, ed., *Bernhard von Clairvaux, Mönch und Mystiker: Internationaler Bernhardkongress Mainz 1953* (Wiesbaden: F. Steiner, 1955). Charles Dumont, 'Saint Bernard: A Mystic According to the Rule of Saint Benedict,' *Cistercian Studies* 16 (1981) 154-67.
56 Kalamazoo: Cistercian Publications, 1991. See also Michael Casey, 'Bernard's Biblical Mysticism: Approaching SC 74,' *Studies in Spirituality* 4 (1994) 12-30.
57 Denis Farkasfalvy has observed: 'It was by no coincidence that at the Congress of Rome in 1990É, the two key-speakers, Ferruccio Gastaldelli, in his opening speech, and Jean Leclercq, in his concluding remarks, returned to this same issue of how to qualify St. Bernard's theology and St. Bernard himself as a theologian. The terms were again, on the one hand, "mystical theology," as employed by Gilson and "monastic theology," as used and popularized by Leclercq in 1953 and thereafter.' Denis Farkasfalvy,

'Bernard's Concept of the Spiritual Life,' *Analecta Cisterciensia* 53 (1997) 3-14, here 4. I prefer the expression 'monastic theology'; for a description of it, see Posset, *Pater Bernhardus*, 91-95. See also Ulrich Köpf, 'Ein Modell religiöser Erfahrung in der monastischen Theologie: Bernhard von Clairvaux,' in Walter Haug and Dietmar Mieth, eds., *Religiöse Erfahrung. Historische Modelle in christlicher Tradition* (Munich: Wilhelm Fink Verlag, 1992) 109-23; Kent Emery, Jr., *Monastic, Scholastic and Mystical Theologies from the Later Middle Ages* (Aldershot, UK: Ashgate, 1997).

58 See Leclercq, 'Toward a Sociological Interpretation,' 21.

59 Very dramatically Bernard says, with Saint Jerome's words, that 'the duty of a monk is not to teach but to weep': *Et scimus monachi officium non docere esse, sed lugere.... Certum est quod publice praedicare nec monacho convenit*, SC 64.3, SBOp 2:168,3-6. He is quoting Jerome's *Contra Vigilantium*; *Patrologia Latina* 23:351. See on this, Winkler, *Bernhard*, 186.

60 See Hofmeister, 209-273.

61 See Hofmeister, 236.

62 *Nulli monacho parochia regenda committatur*; Hofmeister, 244.

63 See Hofmeister, 268-69.

64 Winkler, *Bernhard*, 24, speaks correctly of Bernard's *Pastoraltheologie*.

65 One of the most recent biographies, by Peter Dinzelbacher (*Bernhard von Clairvaux. Leben und Werk des berühmten Zisterziensers* [Darmstadt: Primus Verlag, 1998] with more than 3000 notes), has come under criticism for not doing justice to Bernard the theologian; see Ulrich Köpf, 'Probleme einer Biographie Bernhards von Clairvaux. Bemerkungen zu Peter Dinzelbachers Bernhard-Buch,' 425 (see above in note 33).

66 Olivera, 9-11.

67 See Winkler, *Bernhard*, 208-210.

68 See Ep 42, SBOp 7:100-131. See Gerhard B. Winkler, 'Bernhard von Clairvaux: Ep 42 de moribus et officio episcoporum: Zu einer Theologie der Seelsorge zwischen Utopie und historischer Wirklichkeit,' in Hans Paarhammer and Franz-Martin Schmölz, eds., *Uni trinoque domino: Karl Berg, Bischof im Dienste der Einheit: Eine Festgabe Erzbischof Karl Berg zum 80. Geburtstag* (Thauer, Tirol: Österreichischer Kulturverlag, 1989) 416-27; Winkler, *Bernhard*, 186-207.

69 See Ep 42.2, SBOp 7:102,17-20.

70 *Episcopale opus curamque pastoralem*, Ep 42.3; SBOp 7:103,1-2. *Ministerium, inquam, non dominium*, 7:103,20. See Winkler, *Bernhard*, 191

71 See Winkler's introduction to vol. 4 of the German/Latin edition, 4:135-38.

72 See Leclercq, 'Toward a Sociological Interpretation,' 24-25.

## Introduction

73 *Sine sollicitudine praelatus*, Ep193,9; SBOp 7:44,16-17. See Winkler, *Bernhard*, 238, 245. Bernard's concept of *sollicitudo* as a bishop's pastoral care is studied by J. Rivière in 'In partem sollicitudinis,' *Revue des sciences religieuses* 5 (1925) 210-31.
74 See Csi 2,10; SBOp 3:417,21-22.
75 *Sonans tibi episcopi nomine non dominium, sed officium*; SBOp 3:417,17-18.
76 *Ad catholicam rediit unitatem*; Ep 132 to the clergy of Milan; SBOp 7:328,19.
77 See SC 80.8; SBOp 2:283,2; Evans, 96.
78 Div 11.1; SBOp 6/1:124,7.
79 On this, see Gerhard B. Winkler's introduction to the German vol. VII of Bernard's works, 27.
80 See Rémi Brague, *Saint Bernard et la philosophie* (Paris: Presses Universitaires de France, 1993); Leclercq, *Maurice Blondel lecteur de Bernard de Clairvaux* (see above note 4).
81 *Saint Bernard Théologien: Actes du Congrès de Dijon, 15-19 septembre 1953* (Rome: Editiones Cistercienses, 1953). Denis Farkasfalvy, 'Bernard the Theologian: Forty Years of Research,' *Communio* 17 (1990) 580-94, points out that a breakthrough in Bernard studies occurred with the Bernard Congress in 1953 and with the beginning of the critical edition of Bernard's works at that time. He deplores the fact that Bernard in theological studies in the 1970s and afterwards have 'not made significant progress' (p. 592).
82 *Bernardus Magister*, the title for the collection of the congress papers of 1990 (see above note 33).
83 See Dennis E. Tamburello, *Bernard of Clairvaux: Essential Writings* (New York: Crossroad, 2000); idem, *Union with Christ: John Calvin and the Mysticism of St. Bernard* (Louisville: Westminster John Knox Press, 1994).
84 See Evans, 48.
85 SC 43.4; SBOp 2:43,21-22.
86 SC 45.3; SBOp 2:51,19-20. See Posset, *Pater Bernhardus*, 248-49.
87 See Div 7.1; SBOp 6/1:108,6-7; see Evans, 48.
88 See Ep 108.2; SBOp 7:278,6-11.
89 See Winkler, *Bernhard*, 208. Elsewhere I have argued that the Reformer Martin Luther became a teacher of pastoral care because of his encounter and high esteem for Bernard's writings. See Franz Posset, 'Lehrer der Seelsorge: Das kumenische Potential der Seelsorge-Konzeption des alten Luther,' *Luther* 72 (2001) 3-17.
90 See Winkler, *Bernhard*, 136.

91 *Quamobrem, si sapis, concham te exhiberis, et non canalem*, SBOp 1:104,19. For a present-day application, see Dominik Nimmervoll, "Wir haben heutzutage viele Kanäle in der Kirche, aber sehr wenige Schalen!": Ein guter Rat des hl. Bernhard an die Predigerinnen,' *Theologisch Praktische Quartalschrift* 145 (1997) 150-54; Winkler, *Bernhard*, 216.

92 *Verum canales hodie in Ecclesia multos habemus, conchas vero perpaucas*; SBOp 1:104,24-25.

93 Farkasfalvy, 'Bernard's Concept of the Spiritual Life,' 13.

94 'Bernhard von Clairvaux: Der Brief als Mittel der Seelsorge,' *Theologisch-Praktische Quartalschrift* 141 (1993) 368-72.

95 Evans, 150-71.

96 See the 1508 edition of his works by Judocus Clichtoveus; see Posset, 'Saint Bernard of Clairvaux in the Devotion,' 313f (with picture of the title page of *Melliflui deuotique doctoris sancti Bernardi abbatis Clarauallensis Cisterciensis ordinis opus preclarum* of 1520).

97 *Suo mellifluo eloquio*; Miss 1.1; SBOp 4:14,15-16. See Bell, *Honing*, 63.

98 See Bredero, 161, with note 49.

99 See Bredero, 195.

100 See Gerhard B. Winkler, 'Die Bernhardrezeption bei Erasmus von Rotterdam,' in *Bernhard von Clairvaux: Rezeption und Wirkung im Mittelalter und in der Neuzeit*, ed. Kaspar Elm (Wiesbaden: Harrassowitz, 1994) 261-70.

101 *Audiendum verbum salutis*; Ben 1; SBOp 5:1,2. See Evans, 57

102 *Sed divinorum librorum sequar auctoritatem; nec prophetare videar de corde meo, sed innitar, quoad porro, testimoniis Scripturarum*; OS 2.1, SBOp 5:342,7-9.

103 SC 74; SBOp 2:240,17-20. On SC 74, see Michael Casey, 'Bernard's Biblical Mysticism: Approaching SC 74,' *Studies in Spirituality* 4 (1994) 12-30; Posset, *Pater Bernhardus*, 94.

104 See Evans, 60.

105 *Qua ratione verba Verbi facta ad animam referuntur...*; SC 45.7; SBOp 2:54,5.

106 Sermon on the triple judgment, Div 32; SBOp 6/1:218,11-12.

107 Charles Cummings, *Monastic Practices* (Kalamazoo: Cistercian Publications, 1986) 9-10.

108 See Jaques Rousse and Hermann Josef Sieben, art. 'Lectio divina et lecture spirituelle,' in *Dictionnaire de Spiritualité* 9:470-96; Barry R. Folmar, 'Recovering "Lectio Divina,"' D. Min. Project directed by Gordon Lathrop, Lutheran Theological Seminary at Philadelphia (May 1990), digested in *Luther Digest* 1993, 50-63; Michael Casey, 'Seven Principles

of Lectio Divina,' in *The Undivided Heart: The Western Monastic Approach to Contemplation* (Petersham, Mass.: St. Bede's Publications, 1994) 3-9; Michael Casey, *Sacred Reading: The Ancient Art of Lectio Divina* (Liguori, MO: Triumph Books, 1996); Enzo Bianchi, *Praying the Word: An Introduction to Lectio Divina*, trans. by James W. Zona (Kalamazoo: Cistercian Publications, 1998); Mariano Magrassi, *Praying the Bible: An Introduction to Lectio Divina*, trans. Edward Hagman (Collegeville: Liturgical Press, 1998); M. Basil Pennington, *Lectio Divina: Renewing the Ancient Practice of Praying the Scriptures* (New York: Crossroad, 1998); Charles Dumont, *Praying The Word of God* (Kalamazoo: Cistercian Publications, 1999).

109 *Monastic Practices*.

110 'An Introduction to the Cistercian Tradition,' in Edith Scholl, ed., *In the School of Love*, 15.

111 See Evans, 61.

112 See Oswald Bayer, 'Oratio, Meditatio, Tentatio: Eine Besinnung auf Luthers Theologieverständnis,' *Lutherjahrbuch* 55 (1988) 7-59; Kenneth Hagen, *Luther's Approach to Scripture as seen in his 'Commentaries' on Galatians 1519-1538* (Tübingen: J.C.B. Mohr, 1993); Kenneth Hagen, 'Luther, Martin (1483-1546),' in Donald K. McKim, ed., *Historical Handbook of Major Biblical Interpreters* (Downers Grove: Inter-Varsity Press, 1998); Posset, *Pater Bernhardus*, 132-50; Timothy Maschke, 'Contemporaneity: A Hermeneutical Perspective in Martin Luther's Work,' in Timothy Maschke, Franz Posset, and Joan Skocir, eds., *Ad fontes Lutheri; Toward the Recovery of the Real Luther: Essays in Honor of Kenneth Hagen's Sixty-Fifth Birthday* (Milwaukee: Marquette University Press, 2001) 165-82. As to Luther, one needs to note that he did not so much oppose Scripture and Tradition, but biblical theology and Aristotelian philosophical theology. In general, see on this, Risto Saarinen, 'The Word of God in Luther's Theology,' *Lutheran Quarterly* 4 (1990) 31-44.

113 See Karl Heinz zur Mühlen, 'Mystik des Wortes: Über die Bedeutung mystischen Denkens für Luthers Lehre von der Rechtfertigung des Sünders,' *Zeitwende* 52 (1981) 206-25.

114 See Friedrich Beisser, 'Luthers Schriftverständnis,' in Peter Manns, ed., *Reformator und Vater im Glauben* (Stuttgart: Franz Steiner Verlag, Wiesbaden GMBH, 1985) 25-37.

115 See Franz Posset, *Luther's Catholic Christology According to his Johannine Lectures of 1527* (Milwaukee: Northwestern Publishing House, 1988) 153-57; Posset, 'Bible Reading "With Closed Eyes" in the Monastic Tradition: An Overlooked Aspect of Martin Luther's Hermeneutics,' *The American Benedictine Review* 38 (1987) 293-306.

116 See Winkler, *Bernhard*, 59, 78, 262 (on reforming the Church), Bernard being a disciple of Stephan Harding (died1133) in this regard.
117 See the prefatory remarks in his Ep 77, SBOp 7:184,18-19.
118 *Haurire etiam de manifestis rivulis Scripturarum, et ex eis singulorum necessitatibus inservire.... Est nimirum aqua sapientiae salutis sermo divinus*; SC 22.2, SBOp 1:130,16-20.
119 Ibid., line 29.
120 See *In Praise of the New Knighthood*, trans. Conrad Greenia (revised edition, Kalamazoo: Cistercian Publications, 2001); see Winkler, *Bernhard*, 105.
121 See Posset, *Pater Bernhardus*, 366-77.

# 1. Know yourself

Fig. 6 Reliquary, *Amplexus* in left roundel,
originally from Upper Italy, c. 1575

# 1. Know yourself

### As the motto of the Greeks advises
I am much concerned to know myself, as the motto of the Greeks advises, so that 'I also may know,' as the prophet says, 'what is wanting in me' [Ps 38,5].

From: *Sermon 23 on the Canticle*, no. 9.

### The motto that has fallen from heaven and the insight of Epicurus
The first path and the first step...is knowledge of self. From heaven fell this sentence: 'Man, know yourself' [Oracle of Delphi].... 'The knowledge of sin is the beginning of salvation' [Epicurus].

From: *Sermon 40 on diverse subjects*, no. 3.

### 'O God, let me know me and let me know you'
Your entire free time should be spent on the twofold consideration for which Saint [Augustine, *Soliloquy*] prayed: 'O God, let me know me and let me know you'.

From: *Sermon 2 on diverse subjects*, no. 1.

### 'If you do not know yourself...'
If you do not know yourself, you are like a builder who builds without a foundation, raising not a structure but a ruin....Therefore, let your consideration begin and end with yourself....To yourself you are the first and the last.

From: *On Consideration*, Book II,6.

### The insight of saints
I brought a mirror. A dirty face may recognize itself in it.... A rare statement is this: 'I have nothing on my conscience' [1 Cor 4:4]. You are more careful in your good way of life, if the evil things are also not concealed. Therefore, as I said, you should know yourself, so that you may enjoy a good conscience in the midst of the troubles which you will not lack; more yet, so that you know what you lack. For who does not lack something? Everything is lacking in the one

who thinks that he lacks nothing.... 'It is not that I have already reached the goal or that I would be perfect' [Phil 3:12], and further, 'I do not think that I have reached it' [Phil 3:13]. This is the insight of the saints which is far removed from that which makes someone haughty [see Prov 9:10].

From: *On Consideration*, Book II,14.

### Ignorance of self and the devil's sin

See how great the evil that springs from our want of self-knowledge: nothing less than the devil's sin and the beginning of every sin, pride [Sir 10:15].... For the present it suffices that each one has been warned about want of self-knowledge, not only by means of my sermon but also by the goodness of the Bridegroom of the Church, our Lord Jesus Christ, who is God, blessed for ever. Amen.

From: *Sermon 37 on the Canticle*, no. 7.

### I had no idea; I thought I was sound

The First Adam dressed himself with clothing of pelts, the Second [Adam] is wrapped in swaddling clothes. This is not the decision of the world: either [Christ] is wrong or the world errs. That divine wisdom is wrong is an impossibility. Therefore, with right the wisdom of the flesh is the enemy of God, it leads to death (Rom 8:7) ....

Brothers, Christ's tears bring on in me both shame and agony. There was I playing outside in the square, while in the secrecy of the royal bedroom a death sentence was brought against me. His only Begotten heard of it; he came out; he laid down his diadem; he put on a sackcloth; his head was spattered with ash; he was barefoot, weeping and wailing, because his little slave-boy had been condemned to death. I see him suddenly come forth. I am struck dumb by this new development, I am told the reason why, and I listen. What am I to do? Play on, make play of his tears? Clearly, if I am insane, if I am not of sound mind, I will not follow him, will not weep with his weeping. This is the shame I felt. Agony and fear, how did they come about? I have only to consider the remedy to estimate the vastness of danger I am in. I had no idea. I thought I was sound. Then I found this: the Virgin's son is sent for, the Son of the Most High God, and he is ordered to die in order that my wounds are tended with the precious balsam of his blood.

From: *The Third Christmas Sermon*, nos. 1 and 4.

### Becoming upset by looking at oneself

My advice to you, my friends, is to turn aside from troubled and anxious reflection on the paths you may be treading, and to escape to the easier paths of the serene remembrance of the good things which God has done. In this way, instead of becoming upset by looking at yourselves, you will look at Him and find rest.

From: *Sermon 11 on the Canticle*, no. 2.

### Despair comes from the ignorance of God

Despair, the greatest evil of all, follows on ignorance of God.

From: *Sermon 38 on the Canticle*, no. 1.

### A soul bent out of shape is still capable of the eternal

If, as I have argued before, the soul is great in proportion to its capacity for the eternal, and upright in proportion to its desire for heavenly things, then the soul which does not desire or have a taste for heavenly things, but clings to earthly things, is clearly not upright but bent. But for all, it does not that cease to be great, and it always retains its capacity for eternity. For even if it never attains it, it never ceases to be capable of doing so.... What hope could there be for one who had no capacity for receiving it?

From: *Sermon 80 on the Canticle*, no. 3.

### A soul bent out of shape is no friend of the Bridegroom

[The body to the soul:] Look on me, my soul, and blush for shame.... Blush that despite your heavenly origin you now wallow in filth. Created upright and in your Creator's likeness, you received me as a helper like to yourself, at least in bodily uprightness.... Now, every help you received from me you have turned into disgrace: you abused my subordination to you, you dwell unworthily in this human body, you are a brutish and bestial spirit.

Souls bent out of shape in this way cannot love the Bridegroom because they are not the friends of the Bridegroom, since they are of the world. 'The one who wants to be friends with the world,' he says, 'becomes an enemy of God' [James 4:4]. Therefore, it is a warping of the soul to seek and savor what is on the ground, and it is rectitude to direct from this region one's meditating and desire to what is above.

From: *Sermon 24 on the Canticle*, nos. 6-7.

## Gold under the dirt

Obviously the soul has not cast off her innate form, but has put on an alien one. The latter has been added; the former did not perish, and, although that which has been superimposed has managed to obscure the inborn form, it has not been able to destroy it. ... 'How has the gold become obscured and the finest color changed?' [Lam 4:1]. One laments that the golden [color] is obscured. But the gold is still gold; the original base of the color has not been wiped out.

From: *Sermon 82 on the Canticle*, no. 2.

## We feel about God according to the way we feel about ourselves

[The human soul, however,] cannot feel anything about God or feel God except through her own being.... There are, then four kinds of human beings: the bad, the worse, the good, and the better. Each one feels about God according to the way they feel about themselves.

From: *Sentences* III.124.

## As you have prepared for God so God must appear to you

How great do you think is the grace of familiarity which results from the abode which the soul and the Word share, how great the confidence that follows such familiarity? ... And so it is: God's love gives birth to the love of the soul, and his prevenient attention makes the soul attentive, and his care makes the soul caring. For when the soul can once perceive the glory of God without a veil [2 Cor 3:18], it is compelled by some natural affinity (I do not know which one it is) to be conformed to him, and be transformed to that very image. So, as you have prepared for God so God must appear to you; 'with the saint he will be saintly, and with the innocent he will be innocent' [Psalm 17:26f]. Why not also loving with the loving, spending time

# 1. Know yourself

with the one who has time, paying attention to the one who pays attention, caring with the one who cares?

From: *Sermon 69 on the Canticle*, no. 7.

## Two-fold ignorance: with regard to ourselves, with regard to God

You know well that I proposed for us a sermon on ignorance, or rather on different kinds of ignorance. You remember I mentioned two kinds, one with regard to ourselves, the other with regard to God....

However, I think that first we must investigate if all ignorance is damnable. It seems to me that this is not true....

Perhaps you think that I have sullied too much the good name of knowledge, that I have reprimanded the learned and prohibited the study of letters. Far from it. I am not unmindful of the benefits that the Church has received and still receives from her scholars, be it by their refuting her opponents or by instructing the simple....

All knowledge is good in itself, provided it be founded on the truth....

I wish that before everything else a person should have knowledge of self....

As for me, as long as I look at myself, my eye is filled with bitterness. However, if I look up and fix my eyes on the help that comes from the divine mercy, this joyful vision of God soon tempers the bitter vision of myself....In this way your knowledge of self will be the step that leads to the knowledge of God.... You may see now how each of the two insights is necessary for your salvation, that you cannot be saved if you lack them. For, if you do not know yourself, you will have neither the fear of God in you nor humility. And you will see whether you may presume to be saved without the fear of God and humility.

From: *Sermon 36 on the Canticle*, nos. 1-7.

## No one is saved without knowledge of self and fear of God

No one is saved without knowledge of self; from it comes forth humility which is the mother of salvation, and the fear of the Lord which itself is as much the beginning of wisdom as it is of salvation.... Know yourself then, that you may fear God; know God that you may also love him.... Beware then, both of ignorance of yourself and ignorance of God since there is no salvation without the fear and the love of God. Everything else is indifferent.

From: *Sermon 37 on the Canticle*, no. 1.

**Two-fold knowledge: knowledge of self and of God**

If we have first made sure of this two-fold knowledge, we are less likely to become conceited by any other learning we may add to it. The earthly gain or honor it may confer on us is by far inferior to the hope conceived and the hopeful joy that is deeply rooted in the soul. 'This hope does not disappoint because the love of God has been poured out in our hearts through the Holy Spirit who has been given to us' [Rom 5:5]. This hope does not disappoint because love infuses certitude. Through it the Holy Spirit bears witness to our spirit that we are sons of God [Rom 8:16]....

Just as the fear of the Lord is the beginning of wisdom, so pride is the beginning of all sin; and just as the love of God is the way to the beginning of wisdom, so despair leads to the committing of every sin. And as the fear of God springs up within you from knowledge of self and love of God from the knowledge of God, so on the contrary, pride comes from want of self-knowledge and despair from want of knowledge of God.

From: *Sermon 37 on the Canticle*, nos. 5-6.

**The twin consideration about self; and the heart of God**

Read in the heart of God the testament that was sealed with the blood of the Mediator, and you will find how much that which you possess through hope differs from that which you have in reality. It is written [Job 7:17], 'What is man that you make so much of him?' Great he is, but in him [God], as he is made great by him. Or should he not be great with him who has so much concern for him? As the Apostle Peter says: 'He cares for us' [1 Peter 5:7]; and the prophet says: 'Though I am a beggar and poor, the Lord is concerned about me' [Psalm 39:18]....

What is concealed about us in the heart of the Father will be revealed to us through his Spirit; and his testifying 'Spirit should persuade our spirit that we are children of God' [Rom 8:16]. He may persuade us, however, by calling us and justifying us freely by faith....

## 1. Know yourself

If in this double consideration we now look carefully at ourselves and what we are, namely that in one respect we are nothing, and in another respect we are so great that even such a great Majesty has concern for us and his heart turns toward us, then I believe our 'boasting' [1 Cor 1:31] appears tempered. But by doing this, the boasting may even be augmented and also solidified so that we boast not in ourselves but 'in the Lord' [1 Cor 1:31; Jer 9:23]. No wonder that in looking back at this we can say only this: If he has decided to save us, we will be free at once....

We are it [the Temple of God], I say, but we are this in the heart of God; we are it, but by his grace not by our worthiness.

From: *Sermon 5 on the dedication of a church*, nos. 5-8.

### What is God?

Perhaps you will groan if we ask again what God is, either because we have asked that question so often already or because you doubt whether we are going to find an answer. I tell you, Father Eugene, it is only God who can never be sought in vain [Is 45:19], even when he cannot be found. Let your own experience convince you of that. But if it does not, believe an expert, not myself, but the Holy One who said: 'Lord, you are good to those who hope in you, to the soul that seeks you' [Lam 3:25]. What, then, is God? He is the goal toward which the universe looks forward, the salvation toward which election looks forward; what he is to himself only he himself knows. What is God? Almighty will, most benevolent power, eternal light, changeless reason, highest beatitude, who creates minds to share in his life, gives them life so that they experience him, entices them to desire him, enlarges them to grasp them, justifies them to deserve him, stirs them to zeal, makes them capable of bringing forth fruit, directs them to be just, forms them to become benevolent, moderates them to become wise, strengthens them to be virtuous, visits them for comforting, enlightens them toward insight, sustains them to immortality, fills them to be happy, surrounds them that they may feel secure.

What is God? He is not less the punishment of the wicked than the glory of the humble. He is, as it were, the rational order of equity, unchanging and unbending, reaching everywhere indeed; and every evil which opposes him must be confounded [Wis 8:1].... Righteous is the Lord our God, who deals with the perverse in their own perverse way [Psalm 91:16; 17:27]....

From no scrutiny in heaven or on earth [1 Cor 8:5] would a conscience shrouded in darkness be more glad to flee, if it could. The darkness does not hide even itself. Darkness sees itself and sees nothing else. The works of darkness pursue them [Rom 13:12], and they have no place to hide from them [Psalm 18:7], not even in darkness. This is the worm which does not die [Mark 9:43], the memory of things past. Once it is injected, or, rather, has growing inside through sin, it clings stubbornly, and it is never can be removed. [The worm] never stops gnawing at the conscience, feeding on it, and, since this food is never exhausted, it lives forever. I am filled with horror by this gnawing worm and by such living death....

What is God? The length and breadth and height and depth [Eph 3,18]. 'What?,' you ask, 'are you taking to teaching quaternity now, which you abominated before?' Not at all! .... However, since the search is still going on, let us climb into the *quadriga*, the four-horse chariot.... For we have this instruction from the charioteer himself who first showed us this chariot, so that we might desire 'to comprehend with all the saints what is the length and breadth and height and depth' [Eph 3:18].

From: *On Consideration*, Book V, 24-27.

### Perfect knowledge of the Trinity

Something most sweet in God is the Holy Spirit, the kindness of God [Rom 2:4], it is God itself. If we celebrate the saints' solemn feast, how much more should we then celebrate [the feast of the Holy Spirit] from whom all who were saints derived their sainthood? If we venerate those who were sanctified, how much more appropriate is it that the sanctifier himself be honored?

...Today the Holy Spirit reveals to us something about himself, just as previously we received some knowledge about the Father and the Son. For perfect knowledge of the Trinity is life eternal [Jn 17:3]. Now, however, we know in part [1Cor 13:9]; we believe the rest which we are not at all capable of understanding. About the Father, I know his creation.... But to comprehend his eternity and immutability is too much for me: 'He lives in light inaccessible' [1Tim 6:16]. About

## 1. Know yourself

the Son too, I know by his grace something great: his incarnation.... About the Holy Spirit, I likewise know something, if not his procession by which he proceeds from the Father and the Son, I do know his inspiration.... His procession towards humans began to become known today, and it is now manifest to the faithful.

From: *Sermon 1 on Pentecost*, no. 1.

**No end in seeking God**

[God] must still be sought who has not yet sufficiently been found and who cannot be sought too much; but he is perhaps more worthily sought and more easily found by praying than by discussions. Therefore, let this be the end of the book but not the end of the search.

From: *On Consideration*, final sentence.

# 2. Know yourself as Christ's beast of burden

Fig. 7 Michael Kern, former Abbey at Schöntal, Germany, 1641

Fig. 8 Michael Kern, former Abbey at Bronnbach, Germany, 1642/43

# 2. Know yourself as Christ's beast of burden

**Recognize your origin**

Recognize your origin and blush that you live like beasts of burden. 'Think of your end' [Sir 7:40] and shy away from following the beasts.... With the animals you share the food of the earth because you refused the bread of angels, the heavenly bread. But not only that! What is worse: in an upright body there is a bent down soul. In the [erect] body a similarity to the human soul remains, but in the soul the similarity with God has changed to a similarity with beasts.

...Truly you are created in the image and likeness of God; when you lost the likeness, you became like a beast, but you remain created in his image. Therefore, if in your sublime position you did not recognize that you are slime, you do not want to forget when stuck deeply in slime that you are the image of God.

From: *Sermon 12 on diverse subjects*, nos. 1-2.

**Christ's beast of burden must not be stupid**

Meanwhile, most beloved, glorify and bear Christ in your bodies [1 Cor 6:20]; he is a delightful burden, a sweet weight, a salutary load, even though sometimes he may seem to weigh heavily and even though from time to time he whacks your flanks and whips the laggard, and occasionally even curbs you with bit and bridle [Psalm 31:9] and urges you successfully on. Be like a beast of burden [Psalm 71:21] that carries the Savior [Mt 21:7], but do not be just like a beast.... I know that a likeness to beasts is recommended to humans, but not one that consists in lack of intelligence, or in the imitation of the beast's foolishness but rather of its patience.... Who would not envy greatly that beast on whose humble back the Savior graciously deigned to sit [Mt 21:7] in order to recommend his own inexpressible gentleness...? Be like [his] beast of burden that patiently carries the burden, but that also understands the honor.

From: *Sermon 7 on Psalm 90*, no. 3.

### Be a pious beast of burden for Christ

My brothers, be a pious beast of burden for Christ, and you may say with the Prophet [Psalm 72:22]: 'I was made a beast of burden before you, and I was always with you'. It is you on whom Christ sits since 'the soul of the righteous is the seat of wisdom' [Prov 12:3].

From: *Sermon for the Feast of the Birth of Saint Benedict*, no. 3.

### Consolation for the beast of burden

Would you want us to console our beast of burden a little? We know, of course, that it does not know how to sing. It does not belong to those who can say: 'Your justifications became the theme of my hymns in the place of my exile' [Psalm 118:54]. However, there is one unique thing about it: The Lord is closest to it, when compared to others; not even those who walk close to him are as close as the animal on which he rides.... No one should therefore get upset or despise the one who wants to be Christ's beast of burden....

From: *Sermon 2 on Palm Sunday*, no. 6.

### What do we do with this ass of ours?

And so what will you do when you have insight, and the will is being added to it, but you find you cannot accomplish what is good; when ass-like and bestial impulses follow a contrary law and want to hold you prisoner [Rom 7:23]? What, I ask, do you do about the irrational cravings that are in the parts of your body? .... What do we do with this ass? '[Human beings] resemble foolish beasts of burden, and have become like them' [Psalm 48:13] as their behavior is ass-like, something we have in common with asses. Lord, ascend on this ass [of ours], trample down these bestial impulses, for they must be dominated so that they do not succeed in dominating us.

From: *Sermon 4 on the Lord's Ascension*, no. 12.

# 3. Know your tribulations

Fig. 9 Painting by Anonymous, Cistercian Abbey for women of Seligenthal, Germany; early eighteenth century.

# 3. Know your tribulations

**In the consideration of who we are we become troubled, in the consideration of the Divine we are relieved**

'Within me my soul is downcast; therefore I will remember you' [Psalm 41:7]. The sum total of our spiritual life consists of these two things: [1] in the consideration of who we are we become troubled and filled with sorrow that leads to salvation, [2] in the consideration of the Divine we are relieved and have comfort from the joy of the Holy Spirit.

From: *Sermon 5 on diverse subjects*, no. 5.

**Empty comfort does not bring salvation**

The unhappy sons of Adam have given up striving for things that are true and that bring salvation; they rather pursue worthless and passing things. To what shall we liken the people of this generation? [Luke 7:31]. Or with what shall we compare them? For we see that it is impossible to take them away from earthly and bodily comforts. Really, they are like people on the point of drowning. See how they grasp at whatever comes next to hand, no matter what it is, and hang on to it tightly, even though it be something that can be of no use to them, such as grass roots or something similar. And if it should happen that somebody came to their rescue, they often grip them so tightly as to take them down, so that those who come to help them can save neither themselves nor the others. So it is that they perish on this large and wide sea as they pursue things which are perishable and leave aside the solid realities which, once grasped, could help them rise up and save their souls.

From: *First Advent sermon*, no. 1.

**In all tribulation, 'You, O Lord are my Hope'**

'For You, O Lord, are my hope' [Psalm 90:9]. Whatever must be done, whatever must be declined, whatever must be tolerated, whatever must be chosen, 'You, O Lord, are my hope' [Psalm 90:9].... Because of you I have incurred the loss of everything and counted it as dung [Phil 3:8].... If rewards are promised me, it is through you I hope to obtain them; if a host encamps against me [Psalm 26:3] if the world fumes, if the evil one rages, if the flesh itself lusts against the spirit [Gal 5:17], I will hope in you.

Brothers, to know this is to live by faith [Rom 1:17], and no one can say the sentence 'for you, O Lord, you are my hope' except the one who is inwardly persuaded by the Spirit that he casts his worries upon the Lord, knowing that he will be cared for by him, as the prophet admonishes [Psalm 54:23]. And the Apostle Peter said, 'Cast all your anxieties on him, for he cares about you' [1 Peter 5:7]....God will not abandon those who hope in him. 'He will help them and deliver them and save them, and he will rescue them from sinners' [Psalm 36:40]. Why? By what merits? Listen to what follows: 'Because they hoped in him' [Psalm 36:40]. This is a delightful reason, yet one effective and also indisputable. This surely is righteousness, but one based on faith not on the law. 'They will call to me in any tribulation whatever, and I will hear them' [quoting a liturgical text, i. e., Introitus for the Mass on Thursday after the Third Sunday of Lent]. Look at how many tribulations there are. According to the number of them, his consolations are going to cheer your soul [Psalm 93:19] as long as you do not turn aside to others, as long as you call out to him [Psalm 4:4], as long as you hope in him [Psalm 36:40] and not in any lowly or earthly thing, but take your refuge in the Most High. 'Who ever hoped in him and was put to shame?' [Sir 2:11]. It is easier for heaven and earth to pass away than for his word to become empty promise.

... In every temptation, in every trial, and in any need of any kind whatever, there is an open city of refuge for us, a mother's open bosom. The clefts of the rock [Sg 2:14] are ready, the bowels of the tender mercy of our God [Lk 1:78] accessible.

From: *Sermon 9 on Psalm 90*, nos. 5-7.

## How do we know that God is with us in tribulation?

How do we know that God is with us in tribulation? From the fact that we are in that tribulation. Who would endure, who would hold out, who would persevere without him? We should consider it a great joy when we fall into various tribulations [James 1:2], my brothers, not only because 'it behooves us through many tribulations to enter the

## 3. Know your tribulations

kingdom of God' [Acts 14:21], but because 'the Lord is near to those with a troubled heart' [Psalm 33:19].

From: *Sermon 16 on Psalm 90*, no. 3.

### It is good for me to be troubled

Tribulation is useful that produces endurance; it leads to glory [Rom 5:3-4]. 'I am with you in trouble,' he says, 'I will rescue him and glorify him'. Let us give thanks to the Father of mercies who is with us in tribulation and consoles us in all our tribulations [2 Cor 1:3-4]. A necessary thing, as I have said, is the tribulation which will be changed into glory, as is the sadness which will be turned into joy, a long lasting joy indeed, which no one will take from us [Jn 16:20-24], a manifold joy, a full joy. This necessity is necessary as it brings forth the crown. Let us not be scornful, brothers; the seed is tiny, but a great fruit will grow up from it....The hope of glory lies in tribulation, just as the hope of the fruit lies in the seed....

'I will be with him in tribulation,' says the Lord [Psalm 90:15].... It is good for me to be troubled, Lord, as long as you are with me, better than reigning without you, of feasting without you, of being glorified without you. It is good for me in tribulation to embrace you, to have you with me in the furnace, better than being without you even in heaven. 'For whom have I in heaven but you? And there is nothing on earth that I desire beside you' [Psalm 72:25]. 'The furnace tests gold, and the trial of tribulation tests just men' [Sir 27:6].

From: *Sermon 17 on Psalm 90*, nos. 3-4.

### Pricked on the bed of conscience

None of you need be unnecessarily confounded about past sins, and pricked by them on the bed of his conscience [Psalm 4:4]. Why not? Perhaps you sinned in the world, but did you sin more extensively than Paul? If you have sinned in the religious life, did you sin more than Peter? Yet by doing penance with all their heart they received not only salvation, but also sainthood; they even attained both the ministerium of salvation and the magisterium of sainthood. Do likewise then.

From: *Sermon 3 on the Solemn Feast of Apostles Peter and Paul*, no. 4.

**For who can keep watch over his inward thoughts so closely?**

For who can be a vigilant and diligent observer of his inward thoughts,...able to decide clearly concerning the heart's illicit desires whether they stem from mental disease or from the bite of the serpent?...I certainly have not received the power to distinguish with certitude between what springs from the heart and what is sown there by the enemy. Both are evil, both have an evil source; both are in the heart, though both do not originate there.

From: *Sermon 32 on the Canticle*, no. 6.

### Trouble throughout the history of the Church

I shall try to apply these four temptations in due order to the Church, the Body of Christ....Consider the early Church: was she not most bitterly afflicted by the 'terror of the night' [Psalm 90:5a]? For it was surely night when everyone who killed the saints thought they were doing a service to God. When this temptation had been overcome and the tempest stilled, she became illustrious, and, in accordance with the promise made to her, soon occupied a position as the pride of the ages [Is 60:15]. Disappointed by this frustration, the enemy craftily changed his tactics from the 'terror of the night' to the 'arrow that flies by day' [Psalm 90:5b] by which he would now wound the Church's members. Vain and glory-seeking people rose up, intent on making a name for themselves; they left their mother, the Church, and for long afflicted her with diverse and pervert dogmas. This pestilence was in turn repelled by the wisdom of the saints, as was the first by the patience of the martyrs.

The times in which we live are, by the mercy of God, free from these two evils, but are evidently victim of the [pestilence] 'that roams in darkness' [Psalm 90:6]. Woe to this generation because of the 'yeast of the Pharisees, that is, their hypocrisy' [Mt 16;6], if that can be called hypocrisy which is so prevalent that it cannot be hidden, and so impudent that it does not want to be! Today a foul corruption permeates the whole body of the Church, all the more desperate the more widespread it becomes, all the more dangerous the more it penetrates inwardly....Called to be ministers of Christ, they are servants of Antichrist....Long ago it was predicted, and now the time of fulfillment has arrived: 'See how in peace my bitterness is most bitter' [Is 38:17,

## 3. Know your tribulations 65

Vulgate]. It was bitter at first in the slaying of the martyrs, more bitter in later times in the struggle with the heretics, but now most bitter of all in the [corrupt] morals of the members of the household.... This plague of the Church is deeply rooted and incurable [Jer 30:12], which is why that during peace her bitterness is most bitter.

From: *Sermon 33 on the Canticle*, nos. 14-16.

### Trouble with the unity and plurality in the Church?

To his Bride, the Church, Christ left his own tunic, a many-colored tunic, woven from top to bottom. It is many-colored because of the many different orders that are in it; seamless because of the undivided unity of indissoluble love, as it is written 'Who will separate me from the love of Christ?' Listen how it is many-colored: 'There are different gifts, but the same Spirit; and there are divisions of function, but the same Lord' [1 Cor 12:4 and 6].... [The tunic] therefore should not be divided, but rather remain whole, in an integrity according to its inherited right, because it is written: 'At your right hand stands the queen in a golden robe, surrounded with variety' [Psalm 44:10]. This is why different people receive different gifts. One person is allotted one kind of gift, one another, irrespective of whether they are Cluniacs or Cistercians, or Regular clerics or even faithful lay people. This applies to any Order, any language, any sex, any age, any condition of life, any place, any time, from the first person to the last.

Therefore let us all come together to form one tunic, and let it include us all....

Why wonder at this variety during the time of exile, while the Church is on pilgrimage? Why wonder that its unity, as I may say, is also plurality?....Just as there are many rooms in a single house [Jn 14:2], so there are many different orders in one Church, and just as there are diverse gifts, but the same Spirit, so there are distinctions in the various glories, but only one house. Unity consists in the singleness of love....'He guided me,' it is said, 'on paths of justice for his name's sake' [Psalm 22:3]....

There is not only one path because there is not only one room to which we journey. Whatever path a person is taking, let them not be so concerned about alternative routes that they deviate from the one justice; for by following the path they are on they will eventually arrive at one of the rooms, and so will not be left outside their Father's house.

From: *Apology*, to Abbot William, nos. 6-9.

# 4. Know the Word of God

Fig. 10 Anonymous, Eschenbach, Switzerland,
*Amplexus with Bible at the foot of the cross,* undated

# 4. Know the Word of God

**Lean on the Word**

Anyone who stands and does not wish to fall should not place his trust in himself, but lean on the Word. The word says: 'Without me you can do nothing' [Jn 15:5]. And so it is. We can neither rise to the good nor stand in the good without the Word.

From: *Sermon 85 on the Canticle*, no. 6.

**The Bride of the Word must not be stupid**

What would learning do without love? It would be puffed up. What would love do without learning? It would go astray....The Bride of the Word must not be stupid; but a haughty one is not accepted by the Father either.

From: *Sermon 69 on the Canticle*, no. 2.

**No excuse for ignorance**

Now what excuse for ignorance do we have who are never without the heavenly teaching [religious instruction], never without sacred reading, never without spiritual erudition?

From: *Sermon 6 on the Lord's Ascension*, no. 6.

**The Word of God is golden**

I do truly fear one thing: that the words of salvation [Acts 13:26] heard so many times may begin to become cheap to us because they are just words. A cheap and changeable thing indeed is a human word, of no length in time, no weight, no value, no solidity. It reverberates in the air - hence the word 'verb' - and, like a leaf caught by the wind, it floats, and there is no one who considers it. Let no one of you, brothers, so hear, rather let no one so overhear the Word of God. For it tells you: it would have been good for that person not to have listened at all. God's words are fruits of life, not foliage; but if they are foliage, they are golden. Accordingly, let them not be slighted, not slide away, nor slip by....

These things are being said, brothers, that you may know how readily you ought to listen to whatever pertains to the salvation of souls, how devoutly you ought to receive it, and how carefully you ought to keep it. And it should not be looked at 'as a word of a human being, but truly as the Word of God' [1 Thess 2:13], be it consoling, warning, or even chiding.

From: *Sermon 2 on the Feast of the Apostles Peter and Paul*, nos. 1 and 3.

### From the open streams of the Scriptures

No small effort and fatigue are involved in going out day by day to draw waters from the open streams of the Scriptures and to provide for the needs of each of you....No doubt, the divine word is water of the wisdom that saves, not only by drinking, but also by washing, as the Lord says: 'You are already made clean by the word which I have spoken to you' [Jn 15:3]. The divine power with words, eloquence, assisted by the fire of the Holy Spirit, can cook the crude thoughts of the fleshly person, and turn them into spiritual meanings and into food for the mind.

From: *Sermon 22 on the Canticle*, no. 2.

### If I feel that the sense of the Scriptures is opened to me

If I feel that the sense of the Scriptures is opened to me so that I understand them, or that a word of wisdom bubbles from within me, or that mysteries are revealed through light infused from above, or that the wide heaven opens its bosom full of riches and from on high lets the rain of meditations shower on my soul, then I have no doubt that the Bridegroom is with me. All these are the treasures of the Word, and from its fullness we receive all this [Jn 1:16].

From: *Sermon 69 on the Canticle*, no. 6.

### On the exposition of the precious Scriptures

In the exposition of the holy and mystical words, let us proceed in a cautious [Eph 5:15] and simple way [Prov 11:20], let us follow the way of the Scripture which speaks with our words of the wisdom which is hidden in the mystery [1 Cor 2:7]; while Scripture expresses itself figuratively it insinuates God into our affections. Scripture imparts to us the incomprehensible and invisible things of God [Rom 1:20] by means of notions drawn from the likeness of things familiar to us,

like precious draughts poured into cups made of cheap material.
From: *Sermon 74 on the Canticle*, no. 2.

**When wisdom enters it repairs the palate of the heart**

When wisdom enters, while it dulls the carnal sense, it purifies the intellect, heals and repairs the palate of the heart. Thus, with the healed palate one soon tastes the good, wisdom itself tastes [good now], as there is nothing better among the good things.

From: *Sermon 85 on the Canticle*, no. 8.

**Experience with the Word**

When the Word comes to me as the Bridegroom, as he does sometimes, he never signals his presence by any indicator....

When the Word departs, it is as though you were to remove the fire from beneath a boiling pot. Immediately the water calms down and gets cold. For me this is the sign of his departure, and my soul necessarily feels sad until he comes back. The usual sign of his return is that my heart within me begins to warm again. Such, indeed, is my experience with the Word....

From: *Sermon 74 on the Canticle*, nos. 6-7.

**Let him become to me a visible word**

Let him become to me not an audible word which sounds in the ear, but a visible word that my eyes may see him, a tangible word that my hands may hold him, a portable word that I may carry him on my shoulders. And let him become for me not a written and mute word, but incarnate and living: that is to say, not a word inscribed in dumb characters on dead parchment, but in human form impressed vividly on my chaste bosom, and impressed not by the lines of a dead writing reed, but by the operation of the Holy Spirit.

From: *Sermon 4 In Praise of the Virgin Mother*, no. 11.

# 5. Knowledge that comes from the school of God

Fig. 11 Carlo Garavaglia, *Metal Door with Amplexus*, Milan, 1645-1651

# 5. Knowledge that comes from the school of God

### In the school of the Holy Spirit
Knowledge that comes from the school of the Holy Spirit should taste sweeter to me than that of any teacher in any other school....

So I think that with your hammer you will be able to strike from those rocks something which you would not carried away from the bookshelves of the teachers by using your sharp wits in study, and that at times you will have sensed something under the shade of trees in the heart of the day that you would never have learned in the schools.

From: *Letter* 523, to Abbot Ailred of Rievaulx.

### In the school of piety under Jesus as the Teacher
How much more joy may you scoop from the most serene sources of the Savior....O, if I could ever deserve having you as my fellow in the school of piety under Jesus as the Teacher.... Believe me who is an expert in this: You will find much more in the woods than in the books. Woods and stones will teach you what you can never hear from any teacher. Or do you not think that you can suck honey from the rock and oil from the hardest stone [Deut 32:13]? Do not the mountains drop sweetness and the hills flow with milk and honey [Joel 3:18], and the valleys abound with grain [Psalm 64:14]?

From: *Letter* 106, to Master Henry Murdac.

### Two Teachings from the school of Christ
We are in the school of Christ in which we are educated in two teachings. Some things the one and true Teacher teaches Himself, other things through servants: [he teaches us] fear through the servants, but love through himself personally.

From: *Sermon 121 on diverse subjects.*

### In the school of the Savior
[The apostles] have left everything behind [Mt 19:27], and in the school of the Savior they gathered in his own presence; there they ladled joyfully the waters from the source; they drank the source of life in

this source itself. Blessed the eyes that have seen [Mt 13:16]! But do not you, too, work on something similar, not in his presence, but in his absence, when you listen—though not to the words of his mouth—but to the voice of his messengers?.... In truth I tell you, that you are in the truth, on the right path, on the holy path which leads to the holy of holies.... For your comfort I tell you that from the hands of this sinner the souls of monks, novices, and converse [lay brothers] have flown up to their heavenly joys as free as they were liberated from the prison of our mortality. If you ask me how I know this, I tell you that I was given and shown the most certain signs about this.*

From: *Sermon 22 on diverse subjects*, no. 2.

*Perhaps a reference to a dream or mystical experience.

# 6. Know the true godliness

Fig. 12 Anonymous, former Cistercian Nunnery St. Thomas on the Kyll, Abbey of Himmerod, Germany, 17th century

# 6. Know the true godliness

**Godliness means two things**
Godliness means two things: that we are not presumptuous about ourselves, but perfectly confide in God; that we overcome all impediments of the world through him. We must not loose faith in God, but must act in a confident and trusting manner.
From: *Sermon 54 on diverse subjects.*

**True worship consists of faith, hope, and love**
Happy the person who follows not the counsel of the wicked [Psalm 1:1]. Godly are they who believe in God and love him; for godliness means the worship of God. This worship consists of three things: faith, hope, love, all of which are invisible.
From: *Sermon 72 on diverse subjects*, no. 1.

**Three daughters of a mighty king: faith, hope, love**
A noble and mighty king had three daughters: Faith, Hope, and Love. To them he assigned a distinguished city: the human soul. In this city were three strongholds: rationality, desire, and irascibility. He gave each daughter the appropriate stronghold: the first to Faith, the second to Hope, and the third to Love. He put Faith in charge of rationality.... Hope in charge of desire....Love in charge of irascibility....So the daughters entered their strongholds and tried with all their might to govern and provide for their houses.
From: *Parables* V,1.

**For our spirit is not more present where it animates than where it loves**
'We are saved by hope' [Phil 3:20]. Therefore it is hope which allows us to dwell already in the heavens, while in reality we are still wandering in our bodies on this earth. Or, in other words: we are bound partly to our bodies and partly to the Lord: bound to our bodies by bonds of life and feeling, and bound to the Lord by believing and loving. For our spirit is not more present where it animates than where it loves, unless perhaps unwilling necessity is considered a stronger bond than

free and ardent will. Indeed, 'where your treasure is, there also is your heart' [Mt 6:21].

From: *On Precept and Dispensation*, no. 60.

**Godliness is worship of God**

Godliness is worship of God. Indeed, anyone who loves the world more than God is convicted as wicked and idolatrous, as he honors and serves more the creature than the creator.

From: *Letter* 107,11, to Thomas Beverley.

**He has mercy with our ignorance in praying**

Is the truth of the faith, then, something other than what the Son of God himself promises: 'If you are ready to believe that you will receive whatever you ask for in prayer, it shall be done for you' [Mark 11:24]? None of you, brothers, may hold his prayer in low esteem. For I tell you that he to whom we pray does not hold it in low esteem. Before it has left our mouth, he himself commands that it be written in his book. And we may hope for one of two things without doubt: he will either give what we ask for, or give what he knows is more useful to us. 'For we do not know how to pray as we ought' [Rom 8:26]. He, however, has mercy with our ignorance, and he graciously accepts our prayer, but he does not give us what is either completely useless to us or not necessary to be given us right away. Therefore our prayer will never be fruitless.

From: *Sermon 5 in Quadragesima*, no. 5.

**The hardened heart and God's mercy**

No one with a hard heart has ever attained salvation, unless God in his mercy has taken from him a heart of stone and given him a heart of flesh as the Prophet says [Ez 36:26]. Now what is a hard heart? One that is not torn by compunction, softened by loving-kindness, or moved by entreaty.

From: *On Consideration*, Book I, 3.

**Ingratitude dries up the streams of grace**

Learn not to be tardy or sluggish in offering thanks, learn to give thanks for each single gift. 'Diligently note,' it is said [Prov 23:1],

## 6. Knowledge the true godliness

'what is set before you,' so that no gift of God, be it great or small or mediocre, will go without due thanksgiving. We are even commanded to gather up the fragments, lest they be lost [Jn 6:12], which means that we are not to forget even the smallest benefits. Is that surely not lost which is given to an ingrate? Ingratitude is the enemy of the soul, the destruction of merits, the dissipation of virtues, the perdition of benefits. Ingratitude is a burning wind that dries up the source of loving-kindness, the dew of mercy, the streams of grace.

From: *Sermon 51 on the Canticle*, no. 6.

### Know your gift

A person who has received something and yet does not know what he accepted, stands in the twofold danger of being both ungrateful for the gift he has received and careless in guarding it.

From: *Letter* 372, to Bishop Peter of Palencia.

### True Jewishness does not ignore God's goodness

You will be true Jews if your entire life confesses that you are sinners and that you deserve much greater punishments, but that God is good beyond measure.... Whoever does not ardently desire penance appears by his actions to be saying either that he has no need of penance ... or that penance can be of no use to him, in which case he does not acknowledge the goodness of God.

From: *Sermon 2 on Christmas Eve*, no. 1.

### True Jewishness means confession of sins

Let us find out about the six water jars [Jn 2:6] from which the washing and purification of the Jews, that is those who confess, take place. For if we 'would say that we have no sin, we deceive ourselves, and the truth is not in us' [1 Jn 1:8], which alone liberates us, which alone saves us, which alone washes us. 'If we confess our sins' [1 Jn 1:9], we as the true Jews will have no lack of the jars of purification because God is faithful; he will forgive us our sins and cleanse us from any iniquity [1 Jn 1:9].

From: *Second Sermon after the octave of Epiphany*, no. 6.

**Spiritual life in the cloister is like a second baptism**

You want to hear from me why, among the other practices of repentance, the disciplined life in the cloister has the prerogative of being called a second baptism. I think it is because of the perfect renunciation of the world and because of the unique excellence of the spiritual life. It stands out and above any other human way of life. It makes people professing and loving this way of life similar to the angels, and no longer similar to humans. It even restores the divine image in man, joining us to Christ just like in baptism. We are being baptized so-to-speak a second time as with our spiritual life we mortify our body parts which then are above the earth, and we clothe ourselves again with Christ, being planted anew into the similarity of his death.

From: *On Precept and Dispensation*, no. 54.

# 7. O Lord it is hard, but smart, to be humble

Fig. 13 Anonymous, Abbey of Lichtenthal in Baden-Baden, Germany, 17th century

# 7. O Lord it is hard, but smart, to be humble

### The holy sinner prostrates
O soul, if you are of this [sinful] kind, do not regard as unworthy and despicable that position [at the feet of the Christ] in which the holy sinner laid down her sins and put on the garment of holiness...You may wonder what skill enabled her to accomplish this change or on what grounds did she merit it? I can tell you in a few words: She wept bitterly; she sighed deeply from her heart.... The heavenly physician came speedily to her aid, for 'his word runs swiftly' [Psalm 147:15]. Is not the word of God a saving drink? It surely is, strong and pungent, testing heart and soul [Psalm 7:10].... It is up to you, wretched sinner, to prostrate yourself as this happy penitent did, so that you may be rid of your wretchedness. Prostrate yourself on the ground, embrace [Christ's] feet....Even then you may not dare to lift up a face suffused with shame and grief until you hear him say: 'Your sins are forgiven' [Luke 7:48].

From: *Sermon 3 on the Canticle*, no. 2.

### Self-knowledge and humility
A definition of humility may be as follows: Humility is the virtue by which a person has a low opinion of self on the basis of the most honest knowledge of self.

From: *On the Steps of Humility and Pride* I,2.

### From humiliation to humility
Humility, to which humiliation leads, is the foundation of the spiritual fabric. Humiliation is the way to humility, just as patience is the way to peace, and reading is the way to knowledge.

From: *Letter* 87, to Oger, no. 11.

### Humility, not humiliation
Do you see that humility makes us righteous? Humility, I said, not humiliation. How many are humiliated who are not humble! .... It is not to the humiliated but to the humble that God gives grace [James

4:6].... For the joyful and absolute humility alone merits grace which humility brings to light.

From: *Sermon 34 on the Canticle*, no. 3.

**Pride is the beginning of every sin**

Why is it that of the three Persons whom we confess and adore in the Holy Trinity, it is not the Father nor the Holy Spirit who comes, but the Son.... The coming of the Son could not have taken place without the planning of the Holy Trinity, and if we consider the cause of our own exile then, perhaps we may be able to see, at least in part, why it was especially appropriate for us to be liberated by the Son.

Lucifer, the morning star [Is 14:12], was cast down because he tried to usurp likeness to the Most High, and it was considered robbery to claim equality with God, since this belonged to the Son.... Why are you so haughty, dust and ashes? If God did not spare the revolting angels, what more may he do to you, who are rotten and a worm? [Lucifer] did nothing, accomplished nothing: He merely had a thought of pride; and in the twinkling of an eye he was cast down irreversibly because, in the words of the Prophet, he did not in the truth [Jn 8:44].

My brothers, I beg you to flee from pride; flee as far as possible. Pride is the beginning of every sin [Sir 10:15]. It was pride that caused Lucifer to change so quickly from being brighter than all the stars to being wrapped in eternal gloom.

From: *First Advent Sermon*, nos. 2-3.

**Humility and grace**

Divine grace is always closely connected to the virtue of humility because 'God resists the proud and gives grace to the humble' [James 4:6]. Humility therefore is the answer so that the seat of grace be prepared. 'Behold,' she says, 'I am the maid of the Lord' [Luke 1:38]. How sublime is this humility which does not know how to cede to honors, does not know how to be elated with glory? She is chosen to be the Mother of God and calls herself a maid. Truly it is a sign of no mediocre humility not to forget humility in the presence of such glory.

## 7. O Lord it is hard, but smart, to be humble

To be humble in abjection is nothing very great; but it is great virtue indeed, and as rare as great, to have humility when being honored.

From: *Sermon 4 in Praise of the Virgin Mother*, no. 9.

### Humility and virginity

The angel Gabriel was sent from God into the city [of Nazareth]. But to whom was he sent? 'To a virgin espoused to a man whose name was Joseph'. And who is this Virgin, so venerable that she is saluted by an angel, yet so humble that she is espoused to an artisan? We have here a beautiful alliance of virginity with humility....If you cannot imitate the virginity of the humble Mary, at least imitate the humility of the virgin Mary....You can be saved without virginity, but without humility you can not. The soul that is humble, I say, may be pleasing to God, even if she has to lament the loss of her virginity;...the virginity even of Mary would have no value in his eyes apart from her humility.

From: *Sermon 1 in Praise of the Virgin Mother*, no. 5.

### Humility and faith

I want you to be found always faithful and humble, because both are very necessary for salvation. For the one who gives grace only to the humble is the one who is impossible to please without faith [Hebr 11:6].

From: *Sermon 5 on the dedication of the church*, no. 2.

### The contribution of humility

Humility has its own contribution to the banquet and graces the dish with the bread of sorrow [Psalm 126:2] and the wine of compunction [Psalm 59:5].

From: *On the Steps of Humility and Pride* 2,4.

### I have lived a lost life, O God, but do not refuse a humble and contrite heart

Turn toward yourself, O God, this little that you have granted me to be; accept from this miserable life, I beg you, the years that remain [Psalm 101:12]; but for those years which I lost in my life because

I have lived a lost life, O God, do not refuse a humble and contrite heart [Psalm 50:19].

From: *Sermon 20 on the Canticle*, no. 1.

**Humility in furs is better than pride in tunics**

They say: 'How can these monks be said to keep the Rule? They wear furs, and they eat meat and fat although they are healthy...'. There are people who go clad in tunics and who have nothing to do with furs who, nevertheless, are lacking in humility. Surely humility in furs is better than pride in tunics.

From: *Apology*, to Abbot William, VI.12.

**On the custody of one's heart**

Therefore, the rigor of discipline shall protect you against the flesh; the judgment of your own confession will protect you against the judgment of God; and this [confession] is two-fold: it is public for the [sins] committed in public; hidden for those hidden. For this reason the apostle says: 'If we were to judge ourselves, we will not be judged in this way' [1 Cor 11:31].

From: *Sermon 82 on diverse subjects*, no. 3.

**Thinking about myself; judging myself**

When I can free myself from official duties and engage in a kind of soliloquy with myself, thinking about my being, I consider three aspects of myself, three aspects which are quite clear and immediate. I reflect on the fact that I am a human being, a monk, and an abbot; a human being by nature, a monk as a result of my repentance, and an abbot with respect to the requirements of obedience. Yet I add a fourth aspect which is a matter of grace, specifically that I am also a Christian. This, I emphasize, is a matter of grace, not of nature. If it were a matter of nature, there would be no pagans, no Jews....

I reflect on the fact that I am a human being....While all other animals stoop forward toward the earth, 'he gave each human being an upturned face, so he could look up to heaven' [Ovid]....[God] gave me reason with which to judge myself and examine all my deeds, so that I will not be judged by anyone else [1 Cor 2:15] For as the apostle writes: 'If we judge ourselves, we would not be judged by anybody else' 1 Cor 11:31]. Brute beasts are not damned, therefore, because the power to judge themselves and to examine everything has not been given to them. It has been granted, however, to human beings....I give thanks to you. Lord Jesus. For you gave me myself as a good judge, a kindly judge, a sufficient judge. 'For a spiritual person can judge the value of everything, but can be judged by no one' [1 Cor 2:15]. If I prove a spiritual person in judging the value of things, surely that is enough. For the Lord will not judge the same matter twice [Nahum 1:9].

From: *Sentences* III.125.

## Reasonable judgment of self is part of one's free will

Reason is given to the will for instruction, not destruction....We have life in common with the trees, and sense-perception, appetite, and again, life with animals; it is then what we call the will which distinguishes us from both of them....The consent [of the will], on account of the imperishable freedom of the will and the inevitable judgment of the reason always and everywhere accompanying it, is, I think, well called free choice, having free disposal of itself because of the will and the power to be the judge of itself because of the reason. It is only right that judgment should accompany freedom, as whatever has the free disposal of itself, should it chance to sin, judges itself in the act of sinning.

From: *On Grace and Free Choice*, II,4.

## The book of conscience is being opened

The book of conscience is being opened, the wretched sequence of life is passing in review, its rather sad history is being unfolded, reason is being enlightened, and the surfaced thoughts are being presented to one's own eyes. What is more, these two [reason and memory] are not so much qualities of the soul as the soul itself, so that [the soul] is both observer and observed; positioned to look at itself, dragged into court so-to-speak by these heavy-handed officers to be judged by its own thoughts for the time being....The defendant will not remain hidden from this inner judge.

From: *Sermon on Conversion*, nos. 3-4.

### The three judgments

The judgment is triple: one concerning myself, one concerning my neighbor, one concerning God. A person's judgment against oneself must be severe, against one's neighbor kind, against God pure. A person must be severe in self-judgment. For 'if we would judge ourselves, we would not be judged in the same way' [1 Cor 11:31]. [A person must be] kind to the neighbor, be it that you would talk to him mercifully, be it that you would eagerly and angrily talk to him, in any case, you should do it 'in the spirit of leniency, beware that you, too, do not fall into temptation' [see Gal 6:1]. In purity and simplicity of heart you must attend to the judgment of God, confessing: 'All the works of God are very good' [Sir 39:21]. In this way a person is the strict judge against himself through the insight into the truth, he is kind to the neighbor through the affection of charity, he is pure toward God through the assent of his will.

From: *Various Sermons 8, On Advent*

### The three crosses

...The impenitent thief hangs on the first cross, the penitent thief on the second, and Christ on the third [Luke 23:39-42]. Note, however, that when Adam sinned in paradise, the Lord began to look for him, asking: 'Adam, where are you?'....God shouted 'Adam, where are you?' [Gen 3:9] for a long time but was not able to find him in paradise. So, too, when God came down to earth and finally was hanging on the cross, he looked upon the thief and so-to-speak exclaimed: 'Adam, where are you?' 'Lord,' the thief replied, 'I am on the cross, receiving what I truly deserve [Luke 23:41]. I make no excuse; I earned what I am suffering. I ask for your mercy: remember me, Lord, when you come into your kingdom' [Luke 23:42]. Because he confessed to him, [the Lord] did not impose a sentence of vengeance, but restored [him] to his homeland saying; 'Today you will be with me in paradise' [Luke 23:43].

You will ascend by [your self-] accusation to the place from where you have fallen by making excuses....Because mercy recognizes truth [see Psalm 85:11], she does not allow justice any place to undertake a misrepresentation.

From: *Sentences* III.120.

## 8. Know God in Christ

**What is necessary in order to escape the strict judgment of God?**

We must be very much afraid that, when that time comes, under so exacting a scrutiny much of our righteousness may show up as sin. There is only one thing to do: if we shall have judged ourselves we shall not be judged [see 1 Cor 11:31]. How good the judgment that withdraws me and hides me from the strict judgment of God. I am utterly terrified of falling into the hands of the living God [Heb 10:31]. I prefer to be presented to his angry face judged rather than to-be-judged....I shall scrutinize my ways and pursuits, so that he who will examine Jerusalem with lamps may find nothing in me unexamined or not discussed. For he will not judge the same thing twice.

From: *Sermon 55 on the Canticle*, no. 3.

# 8. Know God in Christ

Fig. 14 Anonymous, *Jesus has jumped from the cross and kisses Bernard*, Chapel on Mount St. Peter, Former Abbey at Heisterbach, Germany, undated

# 8. Know God in Christ

**Longing for Christ's coming**

During my frequent thoughts on the burning desire with which the fathers longed for Christ [and his coming] in the flesh, I am stung with sorrow and shame. Even now I can scarcely restrain my tears, so filled with shame am I by the lukewarmness, the frigid unconcern of these miserable times. We received that grace; but for whom among us does the consummation of that event bring as much joy as the mere promise of it which inflamed the desires of the holy men of old? Very soon now there will be great rejoicing as we celebrate the feast of his birth. But how I wish it were inspired by his birth! All the more therefore do I pray that the intense longing of those men of old, their heartfelt expectation, may be enkindled in me.

From: *Sermon 2 on the Canticle*, no. 1.

**Christ's mediation**

If the mediator is to be acceptable to both parties, equally dependable in the eyes of both, then let him who is God's Son become man, let him become the Son of Man, and fill me with assurance by this kiss of his mouth. When I come to recognize that he is truly mine, then I shall feel secure in welcoming the Son of God as mediator. Not even a shadow of mistrust can then exist, for after all he is my brother and my own flesh. It is impossible that I should be spurned by him who is bone from my bones and flesh from my flesh.

From: *Sermon 2 on the Canticle*, no. 6.

**Your God became your brother**

For thirty-three years [Christ] worked on your salvation on this earth; he was nailed to the cross, condemned to death, subjected to ridicule. Your God became your brother, not the brother of angels, 'for surely he did not come to help angels but rather the children of Abraham' [Heb 2:16].

From: *Sermon 19 on diverse subjects*, no. 5.

## Spiritual advent

Who could doubt the greatness of the cause that prompted [the divine] Majesty to come so far and to descend so low? Evidently it was of great importance since the mercy [shown] is great, the pity much, and the love abundant....

The most kind Savior and Physician of souls descended from on high and tempered his brightness to suit our weakened sight....And, indeed, evening had come and the day came to a close. The Sun of Justice had so far receded that none of its light or warmth touched the earth. For the light of divine knowledge had become very feeble and iniquity was abundant; the fervor of love grew cold....

We now know the person who comes, the place from which he comes, and the place to which he comes. And you know also something about the cause and the time of his coming. One thing remains to be seen: the way by which he comes, and this, too, must be carefully researched so that it may be possible for us to go to meet him as is fitting. It is important to realize that as he once came on earth being visible in the flesh, so he comes daily in the spirit to save the souls of each single person in the midst of the world, himself being invisible....

For this reason it is fitting that, if a sick person has not the strength to go far to meet such a great physician, he should at least try to lift up his head and somehow rise at his coming. It is not necessary for you, o man, to cross the seas, not necessary to penetrate the clouds nor to cross the Alps. I am saying that no long way is indicated for you. You have only to enter into yourself to encounter him. 'For his word is very near you, it is in your mouth and in your heart' [Rom 10:8].

From: *First Advent Sermon*, nos. 7-10.

## The triple advent

There is a third coming, between the two other comings; those who know it delightfully rest in it. The first two comings are obvious, but not the third. For in the first coming, the Lord was seen on earth and went around as a man....In the last coming all flesh will see the salvation of our God [Is 40:5; Luke 3:6] and they will look upon him whom they pierced [Jn 19;37]. The one in between [the third] is hidden; [Christ] is seen within themselves only by the elect,

## 8. Know God in Christ

and their souls will be saved. In the first coming he appeared in flesh and weakness, in this middle coming in spirit and in power, and in the final coming in glory and majesty....This middle coming is, so to speak, the path on which one gets from the first to the last: In the first [coming] Christ has become our redemption, in the last he will appear as our life; in this [middle] one he is our rest and comfort as we sleep among the sheepfolds.

However, so that nobody thinks we invented what we said about the middle coming, listen to his own words: 'If anyone loves me,' he says, 'he will keep my words and my Father will love him and we will come to him' [Jn 14:23]....

If you thus keep the Word of God, you can be quite sure that it will keep you. Let the Son come to you, together with the Father; let the great Prophet come; let him come who will renew Jerusalem and make all things new [Rev 21:5]. This coming will have such an effect on us that, just as we have carried the likeness of the earthling, so we shall also bear the image of the heavenly [1 Cor 15:49]. Just as the old Adam is poured out in the whole person and possesses it all, so also Christ will obtain the entire person. Christ who created the entire person, redeemed the entire person, and he will glorify the entire person, he who healed the entire person on a sabbath [Jn 7;23]. The old man had some influence over us, the disobedient one was in us, in hand and mouth and heart: in our hands through crimes and shameful deeds and in our hearts through desires of the flesh and desires of temporal glory. But now, if there is a new creation in the person, let such old things be by-gone [2 Cor 5:17]. As to the hands, let innocence replace crime and continence replace shameful deeds. As to the mouth, let it speak confession instead of arrogance, edification instead of detraction, so that the old things may pass from our mouths. As to the heart, let love take the place of the desires of the flesh; and let humility counteract temporal glory. And see whether it is not true that Christ the Word of God is received by each of the elect in these three areas: 'Place me as a seal upon your heart' [Sg 8:6] and elsewhere: 'For the Word is very near you, it is in your mouth and in your heart' [Rom 10:8].

From: *Fifth Advent Sermon.*

## They know Jesus, but not as the Christ

We have heard the message, full of grace, worthy to be accepted: 'Jesus Christ, Son of God, is born in Bethlehem in Judah.' With this sermon my soul melts....Be not afraid: Christ is totally sweet and kind, and full of mercy....You must be even happier that he is not a rough physician and that the medication is not bitter....Nevertheless, many flee the physician even today because although they know Jesus, they do not know him as the Christ.

From: *Sermon 6 on Christmas Eve*, no. 1.

## Note that Christ shares his right to the Kingdom with us

And one needs to note that Christ, according to his divinity co-eternal and equal with the Father in everything, did not need this sacrifice [of the cross] for himself, since the Kingdom of God is already his who is God. But as the firstborn brother he wanted for his brothers the kingdom that is his already by his right [being the Son of God]. By the price of his sacrifice he bought the other right to the Kingdom for them. He made this decision because of his wonderful and ineffable love.

From: *Sermon on the Seven Gifts of the Holy Spirit*,
no. 2 (*sermo varius*).

## With the incarnation three miracles occurred

The Almighty Majesty made three works, three mixtures in assuming our flesh, so wonderfully unique and uniquely wonderful that they were never performed anywhere else again in the whole wide world. Indeed, joined to each other are God and man, mother and virgin, faith and the human heart....

The first mixture is excellent, the second is even more excellent, and the third is the most excellent. The ear heard of the first....The eye saw the second... The third entered into the human heart....Note what God has given you in the first mixture, and by what means he did it in the second mixture, and for what purpose in the third mixture.... A remedy was created from God and man which may heal all your infirmities. These two ingredients were mixed in the Virgin's womb as if in a little mortar, with the Holy Spirit like a pestle mixing them sweetly.

From: *Sermon 3 on Christmas Eve*, no. 7-10.

## Most sweet reconciliation: A child is born for us

God is the one who justifies, who then may condemn? ...

After all, he is a little child; easy to appease. Who would not know that a child is quick to forgive? See, if we really only make a little effort, we can be reconciled for very little. For very little, I say, but not without penitence, as our penitence is really a very small thing.... 'A child is born to us, a son is given to us' [Is 9:6].... O most sweet reconciliation! O most sweet satisfaction!

From: *First Sermon on Epiphany*, nos. 3-4.

## O humility, you virtue of Christ

O humility, virtue of Christ, how much you confound the haughtiness of our vanity. All too little do I know, and when I seem to know a little more I soon find myself unable to shut up, being impudently and imprudently pushy and showing off, eager to talk, quick to lecture, slow to listen. And Christ, for how long a time was he silent and lived unnoticed; was it because he was perhaps concerned about inane glory?

From: *First Sermon on Epiphany*, no. 7.

# 9. This is my philosophy: to know Jesus and him Crucified

Fig. 15 Karl Hofreiter, Detail of *Amplexus* with Bernard's Open Book: 'This is my philosophy…' (*Haec mea philosophia: scire Jesum crucifixum* [1 Cor 2:2], quoted in *Sermon 43 on the Canticle*), Fresco Ceiling, Library of the Abbey of Waldsassen, Germany, 1724.

# 9. This is my philosophy: to know Jesus and him Crucified

**Ensure that all your affections, all your actions, are directed to Jesus**

I share in his name, and so I share in his inheritance. I am a Christian, I am Christ's brother. If I am what I say, I am the heir of God, co-heir with Christ....

How shall we explain the world-wide light of faith, swift and flaming in its progress, except by the preaching of the name of Jesus? ...To every place [Saint Paul] brought the good news of Jesus, and him crucified [1 Cor 2:2]....

Talk or argue about what you will, I shall not relish it if you exclude the name of Jesus. Jesus is honey in the mouth, in the ear he is music, in the heart he is jubilation....

For when I name Jesus, I set before me a man who is meek and humble of heart, kind, prudent, chaste, merciful, flawlessly upright and holy in the eyes of all; and this man is the almighty God whose way of life heals me, whose support is my strength. All these re-echo for me at the hearing of Jesus' name. Because he is man I strive to imitate him; because of his divine power I lean upon him. The examples of his human life gather like medicinal herbs; with the aid of his power I blend them, and the result is a compound like no physician can produce....

Hidden in the container of this name, which is Jesus, you, my soul, possess a salutary remedy against which no pestilence will be proof. Carry it always close to your bosom, always in your hand, and ensure that all your senses, all your actions, are directed to Jesus.

From: *Sermon 15 on the Canticle*, nos. 4, 6,7.

**Not a remote deity**

I present him [Christ] as sweet rather than sublime, as [God's] appointed one and not a remote [deity], as the one whom the Spirit of the Lord anointed and sent 'to bring good news to the poor, to bind up hearts that are broken, to proclaim liberty to captives, freedom to those in prison, to proclaim a year of favor from the Lord' [Is 61:2].

Take note therefore of the fourfold anointing, take note of the superabundant and inestimable sweetness of him whom the Father has anointed....He came down to you in your prison, not to torture you but to liberate you from the power of darkness [Col 1:13]. And first of all, as the Teacher of Truth, he banished the murk of your ignorance by the light of his wisdom.

From: *Sermon 22 on the Canticle*, no. 3, 7.

### This little bunch of myrrh was culled from all the anxious hours and bitter experiences of my Lord

You, too, if your are smart, will imitate the prudence of the Bride, and never permit even for an hour that this precious bunch of myrrh should be removed from your bosom. Preserve without fail the memory of all those bitter things he [Christ] endured for you, persevere in meditating on him and you in turn will be able to say: 'my beloved is to me a little bunch of myrrh that lies between my breasts' ....

As for me, dear brothers, from the early days of my conversion, I, conscious of my grave lack of merits, made sure to gather for myself this little bunch of myrrh and place it between my breasts. It was culled from all the anxious hours and bitter experiences of my Lord; first from the privations of his infancy, then from the hardships he endured in preaching, the fatigues of his journeys, the long watches in prayer, the temptations when he fasted, his tears of compassion, the heckling.... The insults, the spitting. The blows, the mockery, the scorn, the nails and similar torments that are multiplied in the Gospels, like trees in the forest, and all for the salvation of our race. Among the teeming little branches of this perfumed myrrh I feel we must not forget the myrrh which he drank when on the cross and used at his anointing at his burial. In the first of these he took upon himself the bitterness of my sins, in the second he affirmed the future incorruption of my body....This life-giving bunch has been reserved for me; no one will take it away from me, it shall lie between my breasts.

From: *Sermon 43 on the Canticle*, no. 1-3.

### This is my philosophy: to know Jesus and him crucified

This is my philosophy, one more refined and interior, to know Jesus and him crucified [1 Cor 2:2]. I do not ask, as the Bride did, where

## 9. This is my philosophy: to know Jesus and him Crucified

he takes his rest at noon, because my joy is to hold him fast where he lies between my breasts. I do not ask where he rests at noon for I see him on the cross as my savior.

From: *Sermon 43 on the Canticle*, no. 4.

### I desire to know nothing more than Jesus and him crucified

'This is a rare bird on earth,' where neither innocence is lost nor humility excluded by innocence.... 'My beloved is to me a little bundle of myrrh that lies between my breasts' [Sg 1:12]....It is enough for me; I desire to know nothing more than Jesus and him crucified [1 Cor 2:2].

From: *Sermon 45 on the Canticle*, no. 3.

### Christ Alone

Christ alone, 'the Wisdom of God' [1 Cor 1:24], is 'the tree of life [Gen 2;9], he alone the 'living bread' which comes down from heaven' [Jn 6:51] and gives life to the world....There is only one 'author of life' [Acts 3:5], 'one mediator between God and men, the man Christ Jesus' [1 Tim 2:5].

From: *Sermon 48 on the Canticle*, no. 5.

### The hidden God

This then is how the Bridegroom stands behind the wall and looks through the windows and lattices....His standing behind the wall then means that his abject weakness was revealed in the flesh, while that which stood erect in him was hidden by the flesh; the man revealed and the hidden God [Is 45:15] are one and the same.

From: *Sermon 56 on the Canticle*, no. 2.

### Christ is the Rock, the clefts are his wounds; I remember the wounds of the Lord

'Arise my love, my Bride, and come' [Sg 2:13]. The Bridegroom draws attention to the greatness of his love by repeating words of love....He shows his concern for the salvation of souls....

And when you consider the lovers themselves, think not of a man and a woman but of the Word and the soul....Nor must you think of the clefts of the rock and the crannies of the wall as hiding places for the wicked....

Another writer has expounded this text and interprets the clefts of the rock as the wounds of Christ. Quite correctly; for Christ is the rock [1 Cor 10:4]...

The wise man builds his house upon a rock....

The rock, with its firmness and security, is in heaven....And really, where is there sure and firm rest for the infirm except in the Savior's wounds? There the security of my dwelling depends on the greatness of his saving power. The world rages, the body oppresses, the devil lays his snare. I do not fall, because I am founded on a firm rock. I have sinned gravely: my conscience is disturbed, but not perturbed, because I shall remember the wounds of the Lord. For 'he was wounded for my transgressions' [Is 53:5]. What sin is so deadly as not to be forgiven in the death of Christ? ...

As for me, whatever is lacking in my own resources I appropriate for myself from the heart of the Lord, which overflows with mercy. And there is no lack of clefts by which they flow out. They pierced his hands and his feet, they gored his side with a lance, and through these fissures I can suck honey from the rock and oil from the hardest stone [Deut 32:13], that is, 'taste and see that the Lord is sweet' [Psalm 33:9]....

My merit therefore is the mercy of the lord. Surely I am not devoid of merit as long as he is not devoid of mercy...Where failings abounded, grace abounded all the more [Rom 5:20]....'Lord, I will be mindful of your righteousness only' [Psalm 70:16]. For this [righteousness] is also mine, since God has made you my righteousness [1 Cor 1:30]. Ought I be afraid that the one will not be enough for us both? No, this is not the short cloak that cannot cover two to which the prophet [Is 28:20] referred. 'Your righteousness is an everlasting righteousness' [Psalm 118:142]. What is longer than eternity? A righteousness that is ample and everlasting will amply cover both you and me. In me indeed it covers a multitude of sins [James 5:20]; but in you, Lord, what if not a treasure of loving-kindness, a wealth of goodness [Rom 2:4]. These are stored up for me in the clefts of the rock....What an abundance of sweetness is here, what fullness of grace, what perfection of virtue!

## 9. This is my philosophy: to know Jesus and him Crucified

I will go then to these storerooms so richly endowed; taking the prophet's advice [Jer 48:28] I shall leave the cities and dwell in the rock. I shall be as the dove nesting in the highest point of the cleft, so that like Moses in his cleft of the rock I may be able to see at least the back of the Lord as he passes by [Ex 33:22-23]....

From: *Sermon 61 on the Canticle*, no. 1-6.

### But so sweet on the cross

This contemplation of his back is no small favor, not to be despised. Let Herod despise him; but the more despicable he shows himself to Herod, the less I shall despise him. For this view of the Lord's back holds something that delights. Who knows whether God will turn and forgive [Joel 2:14], and leave a blessing behind him? There will be a time when he will show his face and we shall be saved [Psalm 79:4]. But meantime may he meet us with blessings of sweetness [Psalm 20:4].... One day he will show his face in its dignity and glory, now let him show 'the back' of his gracious concern. He is great in his kingdom, but so sweet on the cross. In this vision may he come to meet me, in the other may he fill me full....Each is salutary and sweet, the one on high and in splendor, the other in lowliness and in paleness....

From: *Sermon 61 on the Canticle*, no. 6.

### Totally sweet and salvific

'I determined that while I was with you I would speak of nothing but Jesus Christ and him crucified' [1 Cor 2:2]. He is totally sweet, totally salvific, totally delectable, finally according to the Bride's word he is totally desirable [Sg 5:16].

From: *Sermon 2 for the Sunday after the Octave of Epiphany*, no. 1.

### The secret of the martyrs

While gazing on the Lord's wounds [the martyr] will indeed not feel his own. The martyr remains jubilant and triumphant though his whole body is mangled; even while the steel is gashing his sides he looks around with courage and elation at the holy blood pouring from his flesh. Where then is the soul of the martyr? In a safe place, of course; in the rock, of course; in the heart of Jesus, of course, in wounds open to for it to enter.... Now that it dwells in the rock, is it any wonder if it endures as rock does? ....The feelings are not lost, they are leashed. And pain is not absent, it is scorned. From the rock therefore comes the courage of the martyr.

From: *Sermon 61 on the Canticle*, no. 8.

## Meditation on the wounds of Christ

What greater cure for the wounds of conscience and for purifying the mind's acuity that to persevere in meditation on the wounds of Christ.

From: *Sermon 62 on the Canticle*, no. 7.

## The grace of the cross and the breaking of the hardened heart

This is the grace of the cross and its strength: 'I live, says the Lord; I do not wish the death of the sinner but rather that he convert and live' [Ez 33:11 as used in the Lenten liturgy]. It seems to me that this is Christ's voice at his resurrection as if he were saying: Whether the Jew wants it or not, 'I live, I do not wish the death of the sinner'. I wished to die for the sinners: I want my death to bring fruit, and abundant redemption at that....

Who may break the hardness [of the heart] if not he who split the rocks at his passion [Mt 27:51]? Who will give a penitent heart if not he who from whom every perfect gift comes?

From: *Sermon 13 on diverse subjects*, nos. 1-2.

## Christ the Lord is a mountain

Christ the Lord is a mountain, a mountain rising and rich. He is a mountain by its height, rising by the bringing together of a multitude, rich in charity. Now see how he draws all things to himself [Jn 12:32], how he unites all things in unity, substantial, personal, spiritual, sacramental. He has the Father in himself, with whom he is one substance. He has the assumed humanity, with which he is one person. He has the faithful soul clinging to him, with whom he is one spirit. He has the one Church of all the elect, with which he is one flesh. And perhaps he seems to have called this union to be carnal; but I prefer to call it sacramental because this notion is more dignifying, especially because the apostle prompts me to do that when he says: This is a great sacrament; I refer it to Christ and the Church [Eph 5:32].

From: *Sermon 33 on diverse subjects*, no. 8.

# 10. Accusation of self; Justification by God

Fig. 16 School of Mathias Wenzel Jäckel (1655-1738),
Marienstern, Germany, 1708-1710.

# 10. Accusation of self; Justification by God

**Free will and grace**
As a result of free choice, to will surely lies in our power, but not to carry out what we will. I am not saying to will the good or to will the evil, but simply to will. For to will the good indicates an achievement; and to will the evil, a defect. Whereas simply to will denotes the subject itself which does either the achieving or the failing. However, it is creating grace that gives existence to this subject. Saving grace gives it the achievement. But, when it fails, it is to blame for its own failure. Free choice, accordingly, makes us willers; grace makes us willers of the good. Because of the willing faculty, we are able to will; because of grace we will the good.

From: *On Grace and Free Choice*, VI,16.

**What is begun by grace alone is completed by grace and free choice together**
The beginning of our salvation rests with God, and is enacted neither through us nor with us. However, the consent and the work, though not originating from us, nevertheless are not without us....

We must, therefore, be careful whenever we feel these things happening invisibly within us and with us, not to attribute them to our own will, which is weak; nor to any necessity on the part of God, for there is none; but to that of grace alone of which he is full....What was begun by grace alone, is completed by grace and free choice together, in such a way that they contribute to each new achievement not singly but jointly, not by turns but simultaneously. It is not as if grace did one half of the work and free choice the other; but each does the whole work, according to its own peculiar contribution. Grace does the whole work, and so does free choice; there is, however, this one qualification: that whereas the whole is done in free choice, so is the whole done of grace.

From: *On Grace and Free Choice* 14.46-47.

## Faith alone and the desire for baptism

Believe me, it will be difficult to separate me from these two pillars, by which I refer to Augustine and Ambrose. I confess that with them I am either right or wrong in believing that people can be saved by faith alone with the desire to receive the sacrament, even if untimely death or some other invincible force keep them from fulfilling their pious desire.

From; *Letter 77*, to Hugh of Saint Victor, no. 8.

## Justification by faith alone

By 'the righteousness that comes of faith' [Rom 9:30], [Jesus] looses the bonds of sin, justifying sinners freely. By this twofold favor he fulfilled those words of David: 'The Lord sets the prisoners free; the Lord opens the eyes of the blind' [Psalm 145:7-8].

It is well known that you [God] give to all freely and ungrudgingly. As for your righteousness, so great is the fragrance it diffuses that you are called not only righteous but even righteousness itself, the righteousness that makes a person righteous. You are as powerful in making righteous as you are in forgiving. Therefore, the person who, through sorrow for sin, hungers and thirsts for righteousness [Mt 5:6], should believe in you who makes the impious righteous, and, being justified by faith alone, he will have peace with God [Rom 5:1]....

[Mary Magdalene] indeed was virtuous and holy, no longer a sinner, as the Pharisee accused her of being. The Pharisee did not know that righteousness or holiness is a gift from God, not the work of man, and that the person is not only righteous, but blessed 'to whom the Lord imputes no sin' [Psalm 31:2].

From: *Sermon 22 on the Canticle*, nos. 6-9.

## The humble accuse themselves

The haughty excuses his sin; the humble accuses [himself], knowing that God will not judge him a second time [Nahum 1:9, Septuagint], and that if we have judged ourselves, we will indeed escape judgment [1 Cor 11:31].

From: *Praise of the New Knighthood*, VIII.14.

## 10. Accusation of self; Justification by God

### Accusation of self - Justification by God

As long as we speak of our iniquities, [God] will justify us freely [Rom 3:24], so that his grace may be praised. For [God] loves the soul which before his eyes and without intermission watches over itself and without dissimulation judges itself. He asks this judgment of us only for our own sake, since, if we judge ourselves, we will not be judged [1 Cor 11:31]. This is why the wise man is critical of all of his own works, scrutinizes, discusses, and judges everything. He honors truth itself, as he acknowledges the truth about himself, and sees all his affairs as they truly are, and makes humble confession.

From: *Third Advent Sermon*, no. 7.

### An alien righteousness is ascribed to the sinner

What could man, the slave of sin, fast bound by the devil, do of himself to recover the righteousness which he had once lost? Therefore an alien righteousness was ascribed to him who lacked his own.... If one died for all, then all have died, so that, just as one bore the sins of all, the satisfaction of one is imputed to all.... Why should I not have someone else's righteousness since I have someone else's guilt? It was someone else who made me a sinner, it is someone else who justifies me from sin: the one [Adam] through his seed, the other [Christ] through his blood.

From: *Letter* 190, VI.15-16, against the errors of Abelard

### God is my Justifier

I only pay attention to Him as the Judge whom I recognize as [my] only Justifier.

From: *Letter* 42.24.

# 11. Know that it is enough for merit to know that merits are not enough

Fig. 17 Anonymous, Cistercian Abbey of Sticna, Slovenia, second half of the 18th century

# 11. Know that it is enough for merit to know that merits are not enough

**All human righteousness is like a polluted rag**
The soul should know itself and be conscious of the truth about itself....
All [human] righteousness is like a polluted rag [Is 64:5].
From: *Sermon 6 on Psalm 90*, no. 3.

**All my righteousness is like a bloody rag before God**
'The Lord is the one to judge me' [1Cor 4:4]. Of course, I am unable to escape his judgment, and if I turn out to be just, I will not raise my head because all my righteousness is like a bloody rag before him [Is 64:5]. There is no one who is just before him, 'except for one' [Psalm 13:3].
From: *Sermon 34 on diverse subjects*, no. 3.

**It is enough for merit to know that merits are not enough**
It is enough for merit to know that merits are not enough. But as merit must not presume on merit, so lack of merit must bring judgment. Furthermore, children re-born in baptism are not without merit, but possess the merits of Christ; but they make themselves unworthy of these if they do not add their own not because of inability, but because of neglect; this is the danger of maturity. Henceforward, take care that you possess merit; when you possess it, you will know it as a gift. Hope for its fruit, the mercy of God, and you will escape all danger of poverty, ingratitude, and presumption.
From: *Sermon 68 on the Canticle*, no. 6.

**In the Spirit the children of God cry 'Abba' and are instructed to do good**
Of what benefit is it to repent of a fault and not to ask for forgiveness? It is necessary that this, too, is brought about by the Spirit who fills [our] spirit with a certain sweet hope through which you may confidently ask [for forgiveness] without any hesitation. Do you want me to show you that this, too, is the work of the Holy Spirit?

Surely while he is absent you will find nothing of this in your own spirit, because it is He Himself 'in Whom we cry, Abba, Father' [Rom 8:15]....

But what does the good Spirit bring about in us that we may do good? In fact it is he who admonishes, moves, and instructs. He admonishes our memory, he instructs our reason, he moves our will. Our entire soul consists of these three....I have said that he instructs [our] reason. Many indeed are admonished to do good, but have little idea of what to do unless the grace of the Spirit is present anew and inspires their thinking and instructs them to carry it out in action, so that God's grace is not in us in vain [1 Cor 15:10].

From: *Sermon 1 on Pentecost*, nos. 4-5.

### The children of God have tears of devotion

These are the tears of devotion in which not the forgiveness of sins, but the benevolence of God the Father is being sought, as the spirit of adoption as sons descends on us, giving testimony to our spirit that we are children of God [Rom 8:15-16].

From: *Third Sermon on Epiphany*, no. 8.

### The divine testimony on grace and good works

'That glory may dwell in our land, mercy and truth have met each other, justice and peace have kissed' [Ps 84:10-11]. 'This is our glory,' says the Apostle, 'the testimony of our conscience' [2 Cor 1:12]. However, it is not such a testimony as the proud Pharisee gave [Lk 18:11-12], who in his deceived and deceiving thinking gave testimony to himself, and his testimony was not true [John 5:31, 8:13-14], but the testimony which the Spirit Himself gives to our spirit [Rom 8:16] is true. Furthermore, I believe that this testimony consists of three [things]. First of all, you must believe that you cannot have forgiveness of sins except through God's indulgence; secondly, that you cannot claim any good work whatsoever except if He himself granted it to you; finally, that you cannot earn eternal life by any works unless that too is given you freely. For 'who can make someone clean who is conceived of unclean semen, except the one who alone is clean' [Job 14:4]? Surely what has been done cannot be undone; yet if God does not to impute it, it shall be as if it had not been. The prophet [psalmist]

## 11. Know it is enough for merit to know merits are not enough

also has this in mind when he says: 'Blessed is the one to whom the Lord has not imputed sin' [Ps 31:2]. Also with regard to good works, it is absolutely certain that no one performs them on his own. For if human nature was unable to stand while still in its integrity, how much less will it be able, corrupted as it now is, to rise [from its fall] on its own? It is certain that all things tend of themselves to return to their origin, as far as they can, and always tend downwards. So it is also with us, since we are created out of nothing, and when left to ourselves, it is an established fact that we always fall into sin which is nothingness.

Moreover, as to eternal life, we know that 'the sufferings of this present time are not to be compared with the glory to come' [Rom 8:18], not even if one person were to endure them all. For human merits are not such that they constitute a right to eternal life, or that God would be doing us an injury if he did not bestow it. Leaving aside the fact that all merits are the gifts of God, so that on their account man is more indebted to God than God to man: what are all merits in comparison with such great glory? After all, who is better than the prophet to whom the Lord himself attested so notably, saying: 'I have found him to be a man after my own heart' [Acts 13:22]? Yet, even he had to say to God: 'Do not enter into judgment with your servant' [Psalm 142:2]. Therefore, 'let nobody deceive himself' [1 Cor 3:18], because if only one had wanted to consider things carefully, one would undoubtedly discover that one cannot 'withstand with ten thousand [soldiers] someone who is coming with twenty thousand' [Luke 14:31].

What we have just been talking about is by no means enough, but ought rather to be taken as the beginning and, as it were, the foundation of faith. So if, then, you believe that your sins cannot be blotted out except by the one against whom alone you have sinned, and to whom sin has no access, you do well; but add to this that you also believe this: that through him your sins are forgiven you. This is the testimony that the Holy Spirit gives in our heart [Rom 8:16], saying, 'Your sins are forgiven you' [Matt 9:5]. For thus the Apostle [Paul] concludes that 'a person is justified freely by faith' [Rom 3:24,28]. This is so also with regards to merits: to believe that they cannot be acquired except through God, is so long not enough until the Spirit of truth [John 15:26] testifies to you that you [actually] have them through God. Likewise with regard to eternal life [Mt 19:16]: you must have the testimony of the Spirit that you shall come to it by divine gift. For God alone forgives sins, God alone bestows merits, and God alone no less gives the rewards.

Furthermore, these testimonies have been made exceedingly believable [Psalm 92:5]. For the forgiveness of sins I hold the strongest argument: the Lord's passion. This is so because the voice of his blood is far stronger than the voice of Abel's blood [Gen 4:10; Heb 12:24], as it proclaims the remission of all sins aloud in the hearts of the elect. 'He was handed over for our sins' [Rom 4:25], and there is no doubt that his death is more powerful and effective unto good than our sins are unto evil. Concerning good works, I have no less effective an argument in his resurrection, because 'he rose for our justification' [Rom 4:25]. Further, concerning the hope of reward, his ascension is the testimony, because he ascended for our glorification. To these three testimonies [on the forgiveness of sins, good works, and hope for reward] you find references in the psalms, as the prophet [psalmist] says: 'Happy is the one to whom the Lord had not imputed sin' [Ps 31:2], and, in another place, 'Happy is the one whose help is from You' [Ps 83:6], and, again, 'Happy is the one whom you have chosen and taken up, who shall dwell in your courts' [Psalm 64:5]. Here you have the true glory, the glory that dwells within us, because it is the glory of the one who 'dwells by faith in our hearts' [Eph 3:17]. However, the children of Adam, 'seeking glory one from another,' did not want 'the glory that is from God alone' [John 5:44], and thus, pursuing the external, fleeting glory, they have had their glory, however not so much in themselves, but rather from others.

From: *First Sermon on the Annunciation*, nos. 1-4.

## Faith and work is like flower and fruit

If however, you want to attribute both these, the flowers and the fruit, to the one person according to their moral sense, understand the flower as faith, the fruit as action. Nor do I think that this will seem wrong to you, if, just as the flower by necessity precedes the fruit, so faith ought to come before good works. Without faith, moreover, it is impossible to please God, as Paul attests [Heb 11,6]. And he even teaches that 'whatever does not proceed from faith is sin' [Rom 14:23]. Hence there is neither fruit without a flower nor a good work without faith. But then, faith without good works is dead, just as a flower seems vain where no fruit follows.

From: *Sermon 51 on the Canticle*, no. 2.

### The death of faith is its separation from charity

The death of faith is its separation from charity. Do you believe in Christ? Do the works of Christ so that your faith will live; love will animate your faith, action will prove it.... You see then that right faith will not make a right man unless it is enlivened by love.... Deeds, however right they may be, cannot make the heart righteous without faith.

From: *Sermon 24 on the Canticle*, no. 8.

### In faith, not works of the law

For you have not chosen me, but I have chosen you [John 15:16f]; not for any merits that I found in you did I choose you, but I went before you. Thus have I betrothed you to myself in faith, not in the works of the law.

From: *Sermon 67 on the Canticle*, no. 11.

### God is the author of all merits

God is, in consequence, the author of merit, who both applies the will to the work, and supplies the work to the will. Besides, if the merits which we refer to as ours are rightly so called, then they are seed-beds of hope, incentives to love, portents of a hidden predestination, harbingers of happiness, the road to the kingdom, not a motive for playing the king. In one word: it is those whom he made righteous, not those whom he found already righteous, that he has magnified,

From: *On Grace and Free Choice*, conclusion.

# 12. Know how to shepherd

Sr. Mechthild Bernart, *Priest's Stole for the Abbey of Cîteaux,* 1998
Fig. 18 (left) Draft of the *Amplexus*
Fig. 19 (center) Finished Stole
Fig. 20 (right) Detail with *Amplexus*

# 12. Know how to shepherd

### To evangelize is to shepherd
Even though you may walk in purple and golden clothing, you must not abhor the pastoral work and care, being the heir of the Pastor [Christ].... To evangelize is to shepherd.

From: *On Consideration*, Book IV,6.

### You are a brother of those who love God
Consider most of all that the Holy Roman Church, over which you preside on the authority of God, is the mother of the churches, not the mistress; and you are not the master of the bishops, but one of them, thus a brother of those who love God, and a fellow of those who fear God. Consider furthermore that you ought to be the model of justice, the mirror of holiness, the exemplar of piety, the protector of truth, the defender of faith, the teacher of the nations, the leader of Christians, the friend of the Bridegroom,...the priest of the Most High, the vicar of Christ, the anointed of the Lord, and finally the god of Pharaoh....He who despises your admonition ought to be afraid of your prayer.

From: *Epilogue* of *On Consideration*, Book IV, 23.

### The threefold question
On the threefold question and injunction of the Lord to Peter: Three times the Lord said to Peter 'Do you love me' [John 21:15-17]. Then feed my sheep: meaning feed them through your life, your teaching, and your prayer.

From: *Sentences* III.41.

### The threefold sacrament
Remember to 'give your voice the voice of power' [Psalm 67,34]. That is to say, see that your deeds accord with your words, or rather your words with your deeds, by being careful to practice before you preach. It is a beautiful and sound order of things that you should bear first yourself the burden you are to place upon others, and so

learn from your own experience how to temper all things for other people....Therefore on these two commands of word and example, understand that the whole of your duty and the security of your conscience depends. But if you are wise, you will add a third, and that is devotion to prayer, so as to fulfill that threefold repetition of the command in the gospel on shepherding the sheep [John 21:15-17]. You will find that you can only fulfill the demands of the sacrament of this trinity if you shepherd your sheep by word, by example, and with the fruit of holy prayer. Therefore, these three remain: word, example, prayer, but the greatest of these is prayer.

From: *Letter* 201, to Baldwin.

**Accepting the mandate from the women**
What did the holy women do? 'They bought spices, that they might come and anoint Jesus' [Mark 16;1]....So let these three women, the mind, the tongue, and the hands, buy their spices. For I think that from them Peter accepts the triple mandate as the shepherding of the flock of the Lord: Feed my flock, he said [John 21;15-17], with your mind, feed it with your mouth, feed it with your work: Feed it with the prayer of the spirit, with the exhortation of the word, with the exhibition of the example.

From: *Second Easter Sermon*, no. 3.

**Who are the watchmen?**
[On Sg 3:2-3] [They] pray a lot for their people....They watch and pray.... Remember how the Lord in his wisdom entrusted the sheep to the first shepherd, I mean Saint Peter, and urged him with such persistence to tend it lovingly....The repetition was not pointless, 'Peter, do you love me?' [John 21:17] in handing over the sheep.... Therefore, give heed, you who have been chosen for this ministry.... The sheep must all be pastured on the Scriptures, which are the Lord's legacy....Good and caring pastors never cease to feed their flock with good and choice examples....

From: *Sermon 76 on the Canticle*, nos. 7-9.

## 12. Know how to shepherd

### The knowledge of the power of opening and closing and of discerning: the keys of Peter

'Who shall teach a person wisdom?' [Psalm 93:10] Is it not you, O Key of David, who opens and shuts to whomever you wish? [Rev 3:7] Without a key, how can one even try to open the doors of the treasure of wisdom and knowledge [Col 2:3], or break in? 'He who does not enter by the door is a thief and a robber' [John 10:1]. Peter then will enter who has received the keys [Mt 16:19]. But he will not be alone, for he will admit me also, if he wanted me, and shut out perhaps someone else if he wanted; he does this through the knowledge and power conferred on him from above [John 19;11].

And what are these keys? They are the power of opening and closing and of discerning who should be let in and who should be kept out. And the treasures are not with the serpent, but with Christ. Therefore the serpent could not give knowledge which it did not possess; however, he [Christ] who possessed it gave it.

From: *Sermon 69 on the Canticle*, nos. 4-5.

### Christ the Rock; Peter the marble column

The Lord gave [Peter] the office of governing when he said to him: 'And I will give you the keys to the kingdom of heaven' [Mt 16:19], so that as the janitor of heaven he would admit those whom he perceives to be suitable, but keep out those worthy of exclusion. For the keys are to be differentiated as 'knowledge' and 'power potential,' with which he must admit the worthy and exclude the unworthy from the kingdom of God. For indeed, a pastor must use great discretion, so that he knows whom he has to loose and whom he has to bind, to whom he has to preach profundities and whom he has to instruct in the basics, as the apostle says: 'I became weak for the weak, so that I could save them all' [1 Cor 9:22]. This is the discretion which is meant by the keys that were commissioned to Peter. For the Pastor [Christ] conferred his own name [that is 'Rock'] upon his vicar when he said: 'You are Peter,' 'You are,' he said, called 'Peter' by me [who is] the Rock; you will be a marble column, 'and upon this rock,' that is upon Myself, 'I will build my Church' [Mt 16:18]. He who was the Rock [1 Cor 10:4] did not want the Church to be founded upon Peter, but upon the Rock. This is so, because the Church's entire release [from guilt] comes from God and not from men. It happened that a heresy grew up, and it was a serious one, in the church of the Corinthians, who boasted about their baptizers, saying: 'I am of Paul, I of Apollo, I of Cephas' [1 Cor 1:12]. Therefore, these people, in ascribing their salvation to men, and not to God, wanted to build upon [other] people. To them Paul replies: 'Was Paul ever crucified for you? Or were you baptized in the name of Paul?' [1 Cor 1:13]. Therefore, God did not want a single prince to be ordained over the others, even though there may be other princes in the Church according to the psalmist's saying, 'You make them princes over the whole land' [Ps 44:17], so that the unity, of course, be kept, the faith of the Church [be kept], and if any discord about the faith were to spring up among the disciples, the authority of the one pastor would bring them back to him as the only one. For if there were two prelates [that lead] to diverse sects, sooner or later the faith would be split. And because [Christ] was the leader, he [Christ] granted him [Peter] a certain principal power proper to him. This is the reason that the sick positioned themselves in the streets, and all were cured by the shadow of him, to whom ampler power has been conferred, which cured the sick by his shadow; and this is the reason that this ability [of Peter] represented something that is in the highest Pastor. There are two Churches, the present one and the heavenly one. In the present one, guilt is washed away, so that the cleansed may be gathered in the one above. The present Church is a shadow of the future one. Both these Churches are represented in Peter. His shadow signifies the present Church, while [his] body [signifies] the heavenly one. His shadow cures the sick because the present Church washes away guilt.

From: *Sentences* III.112.

# 13. Know your direction and your spiritual progress

Fig. 21 Window in Abbey Church Hohenfurt,
today Vyšší Brod, Bohemia, c. 1870

# 13. Know your direction and your spiritual progress

### The sweet Spirit gives us direction
The Spirit is sweet and gentle, bends our will, or rather straightens and directs it more toward his own so that we may be able to understand truly, love fervently, and fulfill [his will] effectively.

From: *Sermon 2 on Pentecost*, no. 8.

### When the Holy Spirit is the director
Don't you see that the one who is guided by the Spirit [Gal 16:25] never remains in the same state [Job 14:2]. Such a person does not always advance with the same facility and one's course is not under human power, but the Spirit is its director who sets the pace as he pleases, sometimes more sluggishly, sometimes more quickly, forgetting what is behind and extending to what lies ahead [Phil 3:13]. If you have been attentive I think you can see that your inner experience is responding to what I am outwardly talking about.

From: *Sermon 21 on the Canticle*, no. 4.

### You will not have scrutinized yourself in vain when you recognize the need for a new scrutiny
Therefore if the winter is past...and the spring-like warmth of spiritual grace indicates the time of pruning.... 'Let us examine our ways and our endeavors' [Lamentations 3:40], as the prophet counsels, and let each one judge his progress, not by finding nothing to reprehend, but by reprehending what he does find. You will not have scrutinized yourself in vain when you recognize the need for a new scrutiny.

From: *Sermon 58 on the Canticle*, no. 12.

### Not to make progress is to regress
Anyone who does not care to advance in all the virtues needs to know that he is standing still and not moving on; yes, he actually regresses, because on the road of life, not to progress means to regress, for presently nothing can yet be in the same state. Furthermore, our progress consists in this; I remember having spoken of it often, that

we should never consider ourselves as having reached the goal as yet, but rather we must extend ourselves to what is ahead and try unceasingly for the better [see Phil 3:13], and leave our imperfection up to view of the divine mercy.

From: *Second Sermon on the Purification of Mary*, no. 3

### Not to want to make progress is to regress

If to strive toward perfection means to be perfect, then it is certain that not to want to make progress is to fall back.

From: *Letter* 254, to Abbot Guerin of Aulpes.

### When you begin not to want to become better, you stop also being good

Nobody can be good more than it would be necessary. Paul was already good, and yet never content. He preferred to extend himself to what lies before him, oblivious of what is behind him [Phil 3:13], eager always to become better. God alone does not want to be better because he cannot be better.

Let them depart from me and from you who say, 'We do not wish to be better than our fathers' [1 Kings 19:4] …. Jacob in his vision [Gen 28:12] saw angels ascending and descending the ladder, but he did not see any standing still or sitting down. There is no standing still on a fragile hanging ladder, nor, in the uncertain conditions of this mortal life, can anyone remain fixed in one position. We have here no abiding city [Heb 13:14] nor do we yet possess the one to come, but we are still seeking it. Either you must go up or you must come down. You inevitably fall if you try to stand still. It is certain that the one who does not want to be better is not even good; and when you begin not to want to become better, then you stop also being good.

From: *Letter* 91, to Cluniac Abbots, nos. 2-3.

### Anyone progressing from good to better is a very rare bird

Your progress from good to better is no less wonderful, no less gratifying, than a conversion from evil to good. It is much easier to find those in the world who have been converted from evil to good than it is to find one religious [monk, nun] who has progressed from good to

## 13. Know your direction and your spiritual progress

better. Anyone who has risen even a little above the state he has once attained in the religious life is a very rare bird on earth indeed.

From: *Letter* 96, to Richard, abbot of Fountains, and his monks.

### Let no one say: I have had enough

A forward disciple is the pride of his master. Anyone who does not advance in the school of Christ is not worthy of his teaching, especially when we are so placed that if we do not make progress we without doubt must fall back. Let no one say: 'I have had enough. I shall stay as I am. It is good enough for me to remain the same as I was yesterday and the day before.' Anyone who thinks like this pauses on the way and stands still on that ladder where the patriarch saw no one but those who were going up or coming down [Gen 28:12]....

Run, brothers, in such a way that you may reach the goal [1 Cor 9:24]. This can happen only if you do not think that you have already reached the goal but by forgetting about what is behind, you extend yourselves toward what lies ahead.

From: *Letter* 385, to the Monks of Saint Bertin, nos. 1-2.

### The more someone progresses the less he thinks that he actually progressed

You may perhaps ask from where or how you could possibly know whether you have received forgiveness. Undoubtedly, the grace of preserving one's humility operates as follows: Divine loving-kindness usually ordains that the more someone progresses the less he thinks that he has actually progressed. For even if he reached the highest step the spiritual exercise, he still has something of imperfection left in him from the first step. Therefore it seems to him that he not even reached the first one.

From: *Sermon 25 on diverse subjects*, no. 4.

### 'Religion is not in the [religious] habit,' you say, 'but in the heart'. I agree.

From: *Apology*, to Abbot William, no. 26.

**Faith and understanding**

As faith leads to full knowledge, so desire leads to perfect love. And as it is said, 'If you do not believe, you will not understand' [Is 7:9], so it can be equally said without sounding absurd: If you do not desire, you will not love perfectly. Understanding is therefore the fruit of faith, perfect love the fruit of desire.

From: *Letter* 18, to Peter the Cardinal Deacon, no. 2.

# Epilogue

Fig. 22 Oil Painting by Franz Vettiger (1846-1917) from Uznach, Switzerland, for the Cistercian nuns at Magdenau, 1882

# Epilogue

In great humility Saint Bernard received his insights into self and God. To know Christ crucified was his 'philosophy'. In the images of the 'Embrace' he is shown as a most devout man venerating the Crucified and being loved by him. From this spiritual experience and philosophy Bernard knew himself a sinner and he adored God in Christ as his Redeemer. The essence of his spiritual wisdom is captured most beautifully in the legend of the 'Embrace' and in the history of this motif with all its artistic variations. Here is the hagiographer's story:

> I know of a monk who once came upon Bernard alone in church, prostrate in prayer before an altar. Then over and above the floor in front of him there appeared a Cross with its Crucified. This most blessed man adored the Cross and kissed it very devoutly. In turn the Majesty [the Crucified] himself appeared freeing his arms from the crossbeam to embrace and enfold him tightly to himself. The monk watched for a while, glued to the spot in a stupor of amazement, but then, afraid of offending his saintly father if seen thus prying into his secrets, he slipped silently away.[1]

Originally, the love of God for the sinner is represented by the crucified Christ as he takes one or both of his arms off the crossbeam in order to embrace Bernard who kneels under the cross. In a woodcut of 1440/65 the Crucified, covered with streams of blood, actually smiles at Bernard as he embraces him.[2] Later in the history of this motif, in one unique depiction, we even see the crucified Jesus jumping from the cross, hugging and kissing a rather perplexed Bernard (painting in the Chapel on Mount St. Peter, former Abbey of Heisterbach, Germany; Fig. 14).

The fresco by Karl Hofreiter of 1724 at the library of the Cistercian abbey of Waldsassen in Germany (Fig. 15) makes an explicit connection between Bernard's 'philosophy' and the *Amplexus*, as the artist has placed an open book between the foot of the cross and Bernard's knee. On the opened pages we read a maxim which Bernard took from 1 Cor 2:2 and employed it in his *Sermon 43 on the Canticle*: 'This is my philosophy: to know Jesus and him crucified'.

Fig. 23 Oil Painting by Falkenbach, Our Lady of Spring Bank Cistercian Abbey, Sparta, Wisconsin USA,, 1930s;
copied from the original painting at the recreation hall in the Cistercian Abbey at Mehrerau, Austria, 1876, by M. Paul Deschwanden.

# Epilogue

Fig. 24 Painting by Sr. Maria Mafalda Baur (died 1972) under the direction of the artist Karl Schleh, Cloister Walk in Lichtenthal, Baden-Baden, Germany, 1936; copied from the original of painting of 1487, attributed to Michael Wolgemut, who painted it for the Augustinian Friars at Nuremberg

Fig. 25 Glas Window designed by Margret Bilger (1904-1971), produced at the workshop of the Cistercian Abbey of Schlierbach, Austria, 1950s. The writing on top of the cross reads: *Du bist der Adler, der in die Sonne schaut*, "You are the eagle gazing directly at the sun."

# Epilogue 141

Only three depictions of the *Amplexus* are known form the nineteenth century. One of them is the glass window in the Cistercian abbey church of Hohenfurt (Fig. 21), today known as Vyšší Brod, Czech Republic; it is to be dated around 1870.[3] The window shows the Crucified with his right arm embracing Saint Bernard, while his left arm is still nailed to the cross. This composition (Christ's left arm nailed to the crossbeam and his right arm ready to embrace Bernard) may go back as far as 1460, when it appeared in a woodcut.[4]

Three hundred years after Francisco Ribalta's famous painting of the 'Embrace' (1582), Franz Vettiger (1846-1917) from Uznach, Switzerland, painted our motif, in 1882, for the Cistercian nuns at Magdenau, Switzerland (Fig. 22). With his style he may have belonged to the Beuron School of Art, which was founded by Desiderius Lenz (1832-1928), a monk of the Benedictine Abbey of Beuron, Germany. Vettiger's painting was recognized by an archivist in a contemporary photograph as being located at the right-hand side altar of the abbey church at Magdenau that is no longer in existence.[5]

The third nineteenth-century painting was created in 1876 by the Swiss artist, Paul M. Deschwanden from Stans, who had been trained since 1840 in Italy by studying the works of Raffael, along with the group of religious artists who settled in the Eternal City in order to recreate an artistic style out of a combination of medieval piety and early Renaissance art. Deschwanden apparently painted his *Amplexus* in the so-called 'Nazarene Style' for the Abbey at Mehrerau.[6] It became the model for several copyists, one of them is known only by his last name, Falkenbach. He copied Deschwanden's painting in the 1930s for the Cistercian Abbey of Our Lady of Spring Bank in Wisconsin (which some years ago had moved from the Milwaukee area to Sparta, Wisconsin) (Fig. 23).[7] Spring Bank Abbey is a filiation of Mehrerau, Austria. With Falkenbach's painting the motif seems to have emerged for the first time in the United States of America, as it was produced in an exact copy of the original composition at the abbey in Mehrerau. In its intimacy this painting bears resemblance to Francisco Ribalta's painting of 1582.

For the most part of the twentieth century, our motif remained as rare as in the nineteenth century. However, in 1936, an oil painting by Sr. Maria Mafalda Baur (died 1972) was recreated at the Cistercian

Fig. 26 Oil Painting by Paul Magar, OIKOUMENE:
The Crucified Christ, Bernard, and Luther, 1986.
Photo: Altenberg Domverein, Germany

# Epilogue

Fig. 27 Bronze Sculpture by Werner Franzen, *The Crucified Bends Toward Bernard* (left) and *Luther* (right). Altenberg Dom-Verein, Germany, 1986/87. On permanent display at the Catholic Church in Altenberg

Abbey for women at Lichtenthal, Baden-Baden, Germany, under the direction of the artist Karl Schleh (Fig. 24). The idea was to produce a copy of the composition from the painting of 1487 that is attributed to the Nuremberg artist Michael Wolgemut, the teacher of Albrecht Dürer.[8] This twentieth-century *Amplexus* by Sr Maria Mafalda Baur was meant as an altarpiece for the abbey church. Today it is located in the cloister walk. Bernard is depicted in a white cowl. The shield in the lower left corner is replaced with the coat of arms of the then Abbess M. Bernarda Geiler of the Abbey of Lichtenthal.[9]

A glass window came into existence in the 1950s (Fig. 25) which was designed by Margret Bilger (1904-1971) produced at the workshop of the Cistercian Abbey of Schlierbach, Austria, with the unique title for Saint Bernard, which is written above the cross in German: 'You are the eagle gazing directly at the sun." With this line Saint Hildegard of Bingen addressed Bernard in her letter of 1146/47.[10] An eagle sits under the cross beam on the right side. The kneeling Bernard, in ecstasy, with his head thrown back in rapture, his eyes closed, stretches out to Christ who bends down from the cross to him with open arms to embrace him. Bernard with his two-fold knowledge and mystical experience is shown us here as the Eagle who with his inner eye gazes at the Sun (Christ).

In the 1980s the representation of our motif took a revolutionary turn in Germany. Now one can observe how Saint Bernard's insights into self and God were perceived as being congenial with Luther's spirituality and theology of the sixteenth century, a fruit of the ecumenical dialogues of the twentieth century. The 'Embrace' has now become ecumenical, as we read the Greek heading OIKUMENE over the *Amplexus* scene that was painted in 1986 by the late German artist, Paul Magar (Fig. 26). The Crucified extends his arms to both the Catholic Saint and the Protestant Reformer. At about the same time, Werner Franzen, also a German, created a bronze sculpture showing the same ecumenical *Amplexus* with Bernard and Luther kneeling under the cross, both about to be embraced by the Crucified (Fig. 27). Their respective emblems are placed by their knees in order to identify the figures under the cross as Bernard on the left and Luther on the right.[11]

# Epilogue

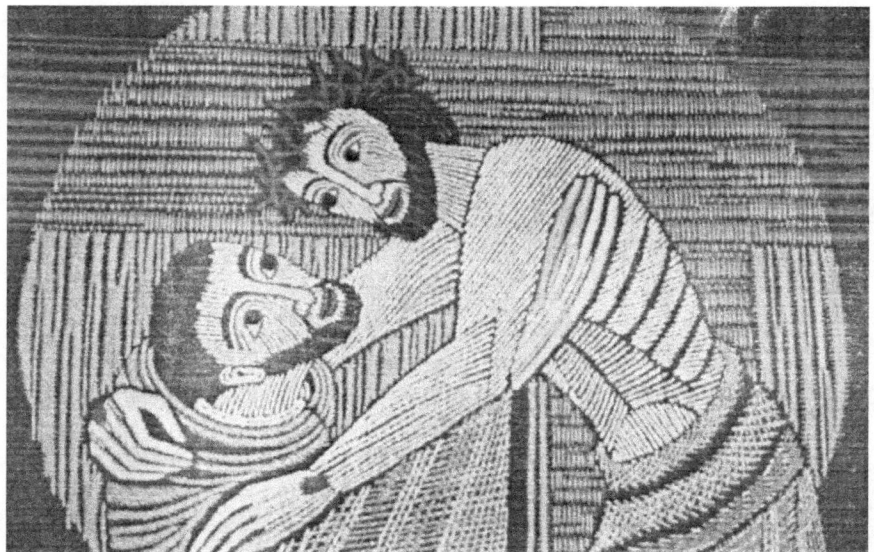

Fig. 28 Embroidered Wall Hanging by Sister M. Lutgera Haberstroh OSF, Reute, Germany;1990, commissioned by Fr. Bernhard OSB, Bad Wimpfen, Germany

For the 900th anniversary in 1990 of Bernard's birth a resurgence of our traditional motif took place, mostly again in German speaking lands. The Franciscan Sister M. Lutgera Haberstroh OSF of the monastery in Reute, Germany, was commissioned by Fr. Bernhard OSB in Bad Wimpfen to use the *Embrace* motif for an embroidered wall hanging.[12] She shows Bernard kneeling as the Crucified embraces him with both arms (Fig. 28). The cross is visible within a bright circle that highlights the upper bodies of the two figures. With Sr. Lutgera's work our typical Cistercian motif found entry into contemporary Franciscan circles, as it had found entry already into Lutheran circles through the representations of Magar and Franzen.

Also for the Bernard Year 1990 Sr. Dr. Mechthild Bernart OCist designed a wall hanging for her abbey, with scenes from the life of Saint Bernard and with the 'Embrace' at its center (Figs 1 and 32). Here, as in the Franciscan wall hanging of Reute, Bernard is kneeling, looking up and reaching out to the Crucified who extends both arms toward Bernard's head, while his feet are still nailed to the cross. However, the two do not touch. Evidently this artist, too, wanted to

Fig. 29 Detail from a hagiographic icon realized by the nuns of the
Monastery of Notre Dame de Bon-Secours, Peruwelz, Belgium, 1990.
Standing Bernard embraces the Crucified
who has not taken his arms from the cross beam

lead us back to the compositions that we see in the earliest depictions of the *Amplexus* in the Middle Ages when Bernard was always shown kneeling and receiving the embrace of Christ crucified.[13]

Also in 1990 the Cistercian nuns of the monastery of Notre Dame de Bon-Secours in Peruwelz, Belgium, created an icon with several scenes from Bernard's life, including the *Amplexus*. However, here we see an eagerly approaching Bernard who embraces the inactive Crucified

# Epilogue

Fig. 30 Glas Window by Edy Renggli, at the
Cistercian Abbey for women of Wurmsbach, Switzerland, 1990

who himself has not yet taken his arms off the crossbeam (Fig. 29). The detail of the icon which shows the *Amplexus* was the model for a line-drawing that graces the second volume of the American edition of the *Early Biographies* of Bernard by Martinus Cawley, OCSO, of Our Lady of Guadalupe Abbey in Oregon, for the 'Centential Edition: 1090-1990.'[14] Another depiction with Bernard standing and reaching out to the Crucified is known to us (Fig. 30); it too was created in 1990, when the Swiss Edy Renggli produced a series of glass windows for the Cistercian nuns of the Abbey of Wurmsbach in Switzerland.[15] In this depiction, however, the Crucified and Bernard have stretched out both their arms for the mutual embrace.

There seems to be no limit to the imagination of the artists. The history of the motif knows Bernard kneeling or standing, and Christ

Fig. 31 Sculpture by Sr. Esther Sawal, OCSO of Santa Rita Abbey, Sonoita, Arizona, for the Abbey of Our Lady of New Clairvaux, California, 1996

with one or both arms reaching out to Bernard, or fully embracing him, or not yet touching him, or jumping from the cross altogether to embrace him, and as in one early woodcut we even see the Crucified smiling at Bernard.

In 1996, Sr. Esther Sawal, OCSO, of Santa Rita Abbey in Sonoita, Arizona, was commissioned by the Cistercian monks of Our Lady of New Clairvaux in Vina, California, to create them an *Amplexus* (Fig. 31). In her sculpture she shows the Crucified no longer nailed to the cross, but sitting on a rock under the cross as he enfolds Bernard tightly to himself. Their faces touch one another. This artist tried to capture Bernard's two-fold knowledge of self and God in Christ, and the intimate relationship of his soul with the mystical Bridegroom Jesus.

The latest known representations of our motif were created again by Sr. Dr. Mechthild Bernart (now abbess of Thyrnau, Germany). One was made on the occasion of the ninth Cistercian centenary, in 1998. The *Amplexus* appears embroidered on the right side of a priest's stole (Figs. 18-20). On the left, we see the Madonna and Child. In this depiction Christ's and Bernard's hands touch each others shoulders, while in her wall hanging of 1990 they do not touch. This stole was a birthday present to the monks of Cîteaux, France, on the occasion of the 900th anniversary of the Order's foundation at that location. The other depiction is found on the abbatial ring for Sr. Mechthild Bernart when in 2002 she became the abbess of Thyrnau. This may be the only *Amplexus* depiction of the twenty-first century so far.

# Epilogue

Fig. 32 Full view of the embroidered wall hanging by Sr. Dr. Mechthild Bernart OCist, Cistercian Abbey at Thyrnau, Germany, for the 900th birthday of St. Bernard of Clairvaux in 1990

Christ apparently always has become and still becomes the center of attention for religious people who deliberate and meditate throughout the history of philosophy, spirituality, and theology and who think about themselves and about God, that is, when they contemplate on their knowledge of themselves and their knowledge of God. This was also Bernard's experience as he developed his philosophy according to which he does not want to know anything but the crucified Christ. Bernard's insight left a lasting impression not only in the hagiography and iconography of him, in particular in the legend that gave rise to the depiction of his experience of being embraced by the Crucified during meditative prayer, but also in his own literary works that are being introduced in this booklet.

## Notes

1 *S. Bernardi Vita Prima*, 7.10; *Patrologia Latina* 185:419. See Franz Posset, 'The Crucified Embraces Saint Bernard: The Beginnings of the *Amplexus Bernardi*', *Cistercian Studies Quarterly* 33 (1998) 289-314; Posset, 'The Dissemination of a Cisterican Motif,' Cîteaux (forthcoming).

2 See Maximilian Pfeiffer, *Einzelformschnitte des fünfzehnten Jahrhunderts in der Königlichen Bibliothek Bamberg* (Strasbourg, 1909) vol. 1, no. 22; W(ilhelm) L(udwig) Schreiber, *Handbuch der Holz- und Metallschnitte des XV. Jahrhunderts*, 8 vols. (Leipzig: Verlag W. Hiersemann, 1926-30) no. 1272.

3 I am grateful to Abbess Dr. Mechthild Bernart OCist of Thyrnau, Germany, for this information.

4 See Schreiber, no. 1276f.

5 I am grateful to Markus Kaiser of the state archive in St. Gallen, Switzerland, for researching the estate of Vettiger in this regard, and communicating his research results to me.

6 I am grateful to Abbot Kassian Lauterer OCist of Mehrerau, Austria, for this information; he also found a note in his archive that this image caused controversy among the monks at that time.

7 See the abbey's webpage with the depiction of their *Amplexus*.

8 Wolgemut's painting is shown in my book *Pater Bernhardus: Martin Luther and Bernard of Clairvaux* (Kalamazoo, Michigan: Cistercian Publications, 1999) 246.

9 The details are taken from the Inventory entry no. PC: K S.26 E 61 of the state of Baden-Württemberg, provided by the Lichtenthal Abbey, Germany.

10 Information and interpretation of this image was kindly provided by Alfred Strigl of the workshop at Schlierbach. See the letter 1 in *The Letters of Hildegard of Bingen*, trans. Joseph L. Baird and Radd K. Ehrman (New York and Oxford: Oxford University Press, 1994) 2 vols, here vol. 1:28.

11 This image was used for the title page of my book *Pater Bernhardus: Martin Luther and Bernard of Clairvaux* (1999).

12 I am grateful to Sr. M. Ingrid of Reute, Germany, for this information.

13 See Posset, 'The Crucified Embraces Saint Bernard'.

14 Lafayette: Guadalupe Translations, 1990. The entire icon is used for the title page.

15 These windows are on display on the abbey's web site.

# List of Illustrations

Fig. 1 (Frontispiece) for the Book cover: Detail of embroidered wall hanging by Sr. Dr. Mechthild Bernart OCist, Cistercian Abbey of Thyrnau, Germany; 1990. Photo: Sr. Dr. Mechthild Bernart.

Fig. 2 From: *Sancti Bernardi melliflui doctoris ecclesiae, pulcherimma & exemplaris vitae medulla...*, Baudeloo, Antwerp: Apud Guilielmum Lesteenium & Engelbertum Gymnicum; 1653. Photo: Zentralbibliothek Luzern, Handschriften und alte Drucke.

Fig. 3 Painting by Freschoz, Cistercian Abbey of Hauterieve, Szwitzerland; c. 1660. Photo: Abbey of Hauterive.

Fig. 4 Painting by Johann Heiß, Castle at Leitheim; c. 1696. Photo: Cistercian Abbey for women of Oberschönenfeld, Germany.

Fig. 5 Painting (Bernard without tonsure) by the School of Altomonte, Cistercian Abbey of Wilhering, Austria; c. 1760. Photo: Abbey of Wilhering.

Fig. 6 Reliquary (*Amplexus* in left roundel) originally from Upper Italy; c. 1575. Photo: Museum für Kunst und Gewerbe, Hamburg, Germany.

Fig. 7 Alabaster Altarpiece by Michael Kern, former Cistercian Abbey of Schöntal, Germany; 1641. Photo: Gereon Ch. M. Becking, Würzburg.

Fig. 8 Alabaster Altarpiece by Michael Kern, former Cistercian Abbey of Bronnbach, Germany; 1642/43. Photo: Staatsarchiv Wertheim, Germany.

Fig. 9 Painting by Anonymous, Cistercian Abbey for women of Seligenthal, Germany; early eighteenth century. Photo: Cistercian Abbey for women of Seligenthal.

Fig. 10 Painting by Anonymous (*Amplexus with Bible at the foot of the cross*), Cistercian Abbey for women of Eschenbach, Switzerland; undated, Baroque time. Photo: Abbey of Eschenbach.

Fig. 11 Metal door with *Amplexus* by Carlo Garavaglia, Cistercian Abbey of Chiaravalle, Milan, Italy; 1645-1651. Photo: Fr. Gabriele Checchi, O.Cist.

Fig. 12 Altarpiece by Anonymous, former Cistercian Abbey for women, St. Thomas on the Kyll, Himmerod, Germany; seventeenth century. Photo: Gereon Ch. M. Becking, Würzburg.

Fig. 13 Painting by Anonymous, Cistercian Abbey for women of Lichtenthal in Baden-Baden, Germany, 17th century. Photo: Abbey of Lichtenthal.

Fig. 14 Painting Anonymous (Jesus jumping from the cross), Chapel on Mount St. Peter, Cistercian Abbey of Heisterbach, Germany; undated. Photo: Gereon Ch. M. Becking, Würzburg.

Fig. 15 Ceiling Painting ("This is my philosophy") by Karl Hofreiter, Cistercian Abbey for women of Waldsassen, Germany; 1724. Photo: Gereon Ch. M. Becking, Würzburg.

Fig. 16 Wood sculpture by the School of Mathias Wenzel Jäckel, Cistercian Abbey for women of Marienstern, Germany; 1708-1710. Photo: Cistercian Abbey for women of Marienstern.

Fig. 17 Painting by Anonymous, Cistercian Abbey of Sticna, Slovenia; second half of the eighteenth century. Photo: Gereon Ch. M. Becking, Würzburg.

Fig. 18-20 Priest Stole by Sr. Dr. Mechthild Bernart, Cistercian Abbey of Thyrnau, Germany; 1998. Photo: Sr. Dr. Mechthild Bernart.

Fig. 21 Glas window at the Cistercian Abbey of Hohenfurt, today Vyšší Brod, Czech Republic; c. 1870. Photo: Sr. Dr. Mechthild Bernart.

Fig. 22 Painting by Franz Vettiger, Cistercian Abbey for women of Magdenau, Switzerland; 1882. Photo: Gereon Ch. M. Becking, Würzburg.

Fig. 23 Painting by Falkenbach, Cistercian Abbey of Our Lady of Spring Bank of Sparta, Wisconsin; 1930s. Photo: Franz Posset.

Fig. 24 Altar Piece by Sr. Maria Mafalda Baur, Cistercian Abbey for women of Lichtenthal, Baden-Baden, Germany (copy of 1487 painting attributed to Michael Wolgemut); 1936. Photo:Abbey of Lichtenthal.

Fig. 25 Glas Window designed by Margret Bilger, produced at the workshop of the Cistercian Abbey of Schlierbach, Austria; 1950s. Photo: Cistercian Abbey of Schlierbach.

Fig. 26 Painting by Paul Magar, *Christ, Bernard, and Martin Luther*; 1986. Photo: Altenberg Domverein, Germany.

Fig. 27 Bronze Sculpture by Werner Franzen, Altenberg, Germany; 1986/87. Photo: Altenberg Domverein.

Fig. 28 Embroidered wall hanging by Sr. M. Lutgera Haberstroh OSF, Franciscan Monastery for women of Reute, Germany; commissioned by Fr. Bernhard OSB, Bad Wimpfen, Germany. Photo: Monastery of Reute.

Fig. 29 Nuns of the Cistercian Monastery Notre Dame de Bon-Secours, Peruwelz, Belgium; 1990. Photo: Monastery Notre Dame de Bon-Secours.

Fig. 30 Edy Renggli, Window at Cistercian Abbey for women of Wurmsbach, Switzerland; 1990. Photo: Jeannette Derrer.

Fig. 31 Sculpture by Sr. Esther Sawal, OCSO of Santa Rita Abbey, Sonoita, Arizona, for the Cisterican Abbey of Our Lady of New Clairvaux, California; 1996. Photo: Abbey of Our Lady of New Clairvaux.

Fig. 32 Embroidered wall hanging by Sr. Dr. Mechthild Bernart O.Cist, Cistercian Abbey for women of Thyrnau, Germany; 1990. Photo: Sr. Dr. Mechthild Bernart.

www.ingramcontent.com/pod-product-compliance
Lightning Source LLC
Chambersburg PA
CBHW070911160426
43193CB00011B/1429